First published in Great Britain in 2017 by A Way With Media Ltd, Shrewsbury, SY3 7LN

Copyright © Andrew Stirling 2017

A CIP catalogue record for this book is available from the British Library.

ISBN 978-1-910469-09-5

Publisher, photographer: Andy Richardson
Design & editorial production: David Briggs
Editorial Assistant: Danielle Colella
Additional Recipes: Steve Brown

Printed and bound by 1010 Printing Group Ltd, China.

www.awaywithmedia.com

Writing a book is not an easy task, but I think all of us owe it to our children, and our children's children, to leave some footprints of our lives. My two eldest sons, Tom and Ben, are old enough to ask the questions but my youngest two, Ollie and Robbie are only 7 and 8, and by the time they start enquiring about my life I will no doubt be departed. So, this is a humble attempt to give an abbreviated version of my life, and I thank all the people, customers, relations and chefs who have in some part contributed.

Andrew Stirling
Wolfscastle

FOREWORD

It is a great honour to be asked to write the foreword for a man whose calm personality, true kindness and willingness to listen and share your problem, has always been available to anybody – preferably over a glass of red.

The hospitality industry is difficult enough but to survive 40 years in the same establishment, against a backdrop of constant challenges is indeed very rare.

I have only known Andy for 37 years, 8 months, 1 week, 3 days, 9 hours and approximately 37 seconds of that 40 years.

His love of the wonderful sport of squash brought us together when he built two courts at Wolfscastle way back in the early 70s. It's where the County Championships were held.

His raising of £80 amongst his keen and enthusiastic members was half of the airfare to allow me to compete in the World Championships in Singapore in 1982, aged just 14. As was usual in those days, the national governing bodies had no funds to develop talent.

One becomes a product of one's environment in life and that experience of being around the best in the world for three weeks set me on my way as a very young man. It resulted in a long professional career as Wales' first true professional player, competing on the World circuit.

I will always be eternally grateful to Andy (and his members) for being an important part of my journey.

World tours would always end with short visits home to Llanelli. Any opportunity to head west to Wolfscastle to see my old mate Andy were swiftly taken.

An infectious smile and incredible hospitality would always welcome me whatever the circumstances: whether the world was at war or not and even if the UK was about to float away into the Antarctic. On every occasion, Andy would turn the conversation around into his real love in life – squash.

Having probably returned from a 5-week tour of 7-hours-a-day, the nonstop goldfish bowl of the sport at international level with press and interviews made it a challenge to listen to Andy talk about his corkscrew serve, skid boasts and reverse angles. He'd developed them and used them time and time and time and time and time again. Hearing about his many, many matches, shot by shot, reached a new level.

And the pressure was only relieved slightly when Doreen, my wife of 32 years , and also a keen amateur player, would visit with me and I could deflect his enthusiasm onto her, whilst proclaiming I had to retire to bed for the much needed professional sportsman's sleep. Little did either know I was simply watching TV in one of the many comfortable rooms. No wonder Doreen became a world class red wine connoisseur.

When not talking to me about squash he would always talk about the other real love in his life: his family and the boys.

So, I for one am looking forward as much as anybody to this book about food, wine, menus and the finer art of delivery and service.

For 38 years, I have been aware that his loyal staff have always known about great service. But as for Andy: I look forward to finding out if he does actually know anything about it, never having had a refreshing break in the conversation about that topic!!!!!!

Andy: thanks for all the support, the fun and certainly, in my post-professional years, the nuclear amount of alcohol consumed when in each other's company.

We send love from Doreen, Hannah, Lewis, Connor and myself: probably the "most visited family to Wolfscastle who never had to pay for anything!!!!!!"

Good luck for the next 40 years. And for all future visitors: an infectious smile, warm hospitality, and wonderfully relaxing surroundings await you. But, whatever you do and whether you used to, currently do, or can even spell the word: don't mention the word Squash. Otherwise your stay could be longer than you expected.

Andy, thank you.

Adrian Davies

European champion. Winner of 18 world ranking events. Top 10 in the world for 10 years. Captain of 'Leekes Welsh Wizards', four times World Championship winners.

Contents

MY STORY

What's it all about?

'When I look back on my little life...' began Michael Caine in his remarkable Hamlet-esque soliloquy overlooking the River Thames, in the classic film of the 1960s, "What's it all about Alfie?"

I am of course not comparing myself to Alfie in any way, morally or otherwise, but you do reach a point in your life where you tend to look back, and ask, "What's it all about?"

The purpose of this book is not to even begin to answer this most complex philosophical question, if for no other reason than to say that unlike Alfie Elkins, I have found peace of mind, which of course is the answer to everything!

No, I have penned it for three main reasons, firstly food, secondly food and thirdly, food! Yes, the love of food, enjoying great dishes and sharing them with others has played a key role in my life.

But there is one further very important reason, let me explain. . .

I am proud to be the owner of the Wolfscastle Country Hotel in Wales. I purchased this rural haven in beautiful Pembrokeshire way back in 1976 and, together with many wonderful staff over the years, worked hard to transform and expand it into the hotel of today.

Recently, British television personality and all-round great lady Davina McCall stayed with us whilst researching for her TV programme 'Long Lost Family.' She was very excited because the episode involved a local person whose mother, some forty years ago, whilst a nun in South America, had got pregnant by a local man and in order to keep the baby had returned to Britain. Her daughter had then contacted Davina and after a major search, the South American dad was found.

This story typifies the fact that, as you get older you want to know who, or what your relations did. Unfortunately, those who have some answers all too often take the information with them without chronicling it.

I have been fortunate that a few of my relations have written books, so I do have some information to hand. Although my mum and dad, who ran a restaurant in Cheshire in the 1960s, were going to write one and call it "A Bra In My Soup" (more of which later), what would have been fascinating to me sadly did not materialise, so I am hoping to fill in some gaps.

So this is a memoir; my aim being to place on record a life enjoyed, one that has been full of wonderful characters, friends and family who have enriched my life. I hope the memories and funny anecdotes I recall here will bring a little warmth and happiness to others.

Finally, back to food! I have been lucky to have worked with so many inspiring chefs – Sally Newton, Rosanne Lloyd, Simon Hopkinson, Marilyn Evans, Mike Lewis, Steve Brown, Alex George, Owen Hall, Tom Simmons, Tom Bennett, Michael Rees, Leon Fitzgerald and Ian Willson to name just a few. I thank each and every one of them for their help and culinary

The Starlings – because of the Scottish pronunciation it wasn't until 1880 that it was realised 'Stirling' was the correct spelling. James Starling was born in 1802 and died 1872.

skills. Through them and my own often flailing search for culinary excellence I have amassed a lifetime of favourite dishes from my childhood and throughout my professional life in the restaurant world. Through this book, I share some of them with you.

Stirling of Africa

My father's first cousin, Dr. Leader Stirling, was a fascinating figure. He spent much of his life in Africa, starting out in 1935 as a missionary doctor. He wrote three books about his experiences.

Leader (and what an alpha male name that is...!) had a most amazing life; building hospitals, starting a scout movement, culminating in 1970 as Minister for Health for Tanzania. The only white man in a black government, he so fell in love with the country that he used to say "My skin is white but my heart is black".

This gave him the opportunity to go behind the Iron Curtain when very few people did – to speak to the Minister of Health for Russia. He also had two private meetings with the Queen.

He died in 2004, aged 97, and I wish I had read his books before he died, so I could have talked to him about his life. According to his obituary in The Times he was related to Sir David Stirling, the founder of the SAS! I was watching a programme on the founding of the SAS and it is amazing that any of them survived. I did meet Rachael Stirling – daughter of

Dibbinsdale Lodge, Bromborough

A wedding at Grandpa's house in 1925. Grandpa in
the back. Granny seated left and Dad and his sister
'Barbie' seated on the ground.

My father, 1914

Dad with Granny & Grandpa

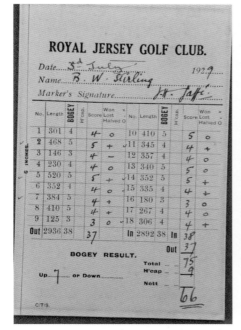

Grandpa was not a bad golfer!

Sister Letty

Archie Stirling, Sir David's Nephew, who is a celebrated actress. She was staying in the hotel whilst on film location down here. Her mother is Dame Dianna Rigg; to older people like myself remembered as Emma Peel in the television series of the sixties – The Avengers. Leader's brother, Uncle John, as a tank commander in the war, liberated Rugle, a village in northern France and has a street named after him, "Rue Major John Stirling" – again, I wish I had asked him about his war experiences. He was asked to write the official account for the 4th/7th Royal Dragoon Guards, which I found a fascinating read.

Another family member I would love to have met was Donald Sorrell, my grandmother's brother. He died in 1958, aged 64, when I was only eight. I remember my mother, saying "Uncle Donald thought he should have been knighted", when I asked why, she replied, "He turned some boat around in New York harbour without the aid of tugs – the tug crews were on strike".

I researched online and discovered that he was the captain of the Queen Mary when he performed this feat. He had also been in the first convoy of the First World War and a captain of a ship in the first convoy of the Second World War and was bombed twice. The second time he pulled up anchor and sailed his boat onto the beach to save the lives of those not killed by the initial bombs. Perhaps he should have been knighted!

1949 and all that

"I was born very young" – I first heard that expression when I came to Wales. It means you are a bit green behind the ears. The other expression I like is when someone dies at an old age and the body just sort of gives up, they say "He died of nothing serious!!!". Anyway, I was born on September 3rd, 1949 in Liverpool exactly ten years after we declared war on Germany. The ravages of war were very evident in Liverpool in the fifties with rows of bomb craters where houses once stood.

My father ran the Liverpool branch of my grandfather's company, Rigby and Evans, a successful wine merchants. We lived in a large house, Dibbinsdale Lodge, in Bromborough, on the Wirral, and the telephone number was Bromborough 1459. I couldn't tell you any other telephone numbers I have had other than my present one. The name derived from the river that ran past the three acres of land attached to the house called the Dibbin.

Granny and Grandpa Stirling as far as I can tell, came from Saffron Walden in Essex. His grandfather, James, had been the mayor. They moved to Bristol at around the turn of the century and in the 1950s were living on the ground floor of a large house, Foyehouse in Leigh Woods, close to the Clifton suspension bridge.

I think my lifelong love of classic cars started in the 1950s as my grandfather had a Jaguar driven by his chauffeur, Joe. By 1959 they had graduated to a Mark IX, very large, all leather and walnut. Joe, dressed in a grey suit and cap, would drive Master Andrew, me, into Bristol to forage for old coins in antique shops.

Grandpa and Granny's first home in Bristol

I had become a numismatist and loved spending hours in antique shops and Joe would drop me at the top of Christmas Steps and wait for my return. Joe and Mrs. Munt, together with Jackie the budgie who never stopped talking, lived in the large basement flat of the house and had the most amazing Hornby Dublo train set – it completely filled a large room. I spent hours "downstairs" enjoying Joe's lifelong creation.

In 1957 I started my five years at "The Leas" – a preparatory boarding school situated on Meols Drive in Hoylake, a seaside town on the Wirral. Aged only eight years and two days, the memory of my mother just leaving me still lives with me. Of course you adapt, but in those days you were only allowed to see your parents three days in the eleven-week terms. The rest of the time you were at the mercy of a mixture of pretty scary teachers, and beatings and bullying were rife.

In the beating department, I had plenty of that, but I can remember on my first night the lad in the bed next to me jumping up and down on the wire sprung bed with metal bed ends. His name was Harding, the nephew of Gilbert Harding, a TV celeb, telling us "newbugs" as we were known, how terrible our lives were going to be. I kicked his bed, he fell, cracked his head on the metal bed end and spent two weeks in hospital! As a result I got known as "mini thug" so for the greater part, was left alone!!

I could see Wales from our dormitory windows and a Welsh speaking friend would throw a

DIRECTORS

D. M. HOLMES
LIVERPOOL

S. LIGHT
BRISTOL

A. J. STIRLING
LIVERPOOL

T. F. HOOD
BRISTOL

W. E. BRAUND
BRISTOL

G. H. BRITTON
BRISTOL

W. H. EDWARDS
LIVERPOOL

A. E. THOMAS
BRISTOL

W. B. HOLLAND
LIVERPOOL

G. W. H. CREIGHTON
LIVERPOOL

F. H. GLAZEBROOK
LIVERPOOL

A. J. KEMP
LIVERPOOL

R. A. FOX
LIVERPOOL

W. P. B. BUCKLEY
LIVERPOOL

H. COLTMAN
LIVERPOOL

J. PRENDERGAST
LIVERPOOL

K. BURGESS
BRISTOL

and STAFF

NG

A. D. WALKER
LIVERPOOL

J. D. P. STIRLING
BRISTOL

M. S. TRIGGLE
BRISTOL

V. MARKS
BRISTOL

J. H. GRANT
LIVERPOOL

A. M. MORRIS
LIVERPOOL

F. R. BURGESS
BRISTOL

E. J. COPSEY
BRISTOL

C. JACKSON
LIVERPOOL

J. McLEAN
LIVERPOOL

A. CRONIN
LIVERPOOL

H. CURRIE
LIVERPOOL

S. O. LEWIS
LIVERPOOL

R. H. JONES
BRISTOL

A. BIBBY
LIVERPOOL

S. M. RODMAN
BRISTOL

A. LEVETT
LIVERPOOL

My Grandfather's staff in 1948 – Dad third in from the left, Grandpa in the middle. Uncle John third in from the right.

**The hat on mum's head that coined the
restaurant name The Hat & Feather**

few of his native words into the conversation. Coupled with that we often holidayed in Wales at Aberporth – where a good friend of my dad, Frank Aspinall owned the Ship Inn and later the Black Lion in Cardigan – thus transporting Wales and the Welsh into my life at an early age.

I stayed at The Leas until I was 13 – the good part was that being capable at sports I developed a love of rugby, football, hockey, squash and golf – all the facilities for these sports being located on the school campus. The food was not bad, other than Spam. I loved the kedgeree, fish pie, apple crumble and grew my own potatoes in my little school garden. The bad news was that many of the teachers were born in the 1800s and the two headmasters, who owned the school, were both alcoholics and hence, it was an educationally failing school. Soon after I left, the school closed and has, like our house in Bromborough, been levelled.

Dad travelled to Liverpool each day through the Mersey tunnel to look after Grampa's company. One story I love is when dad, as a young man, it was probably about 1938, was given the job of entertaining the two sons of Monsieur Martel of the famous French brandy house when they visited Britain. Before taking them "out on the town", they were treated to a meal at one of London's top restaurants, it's still there, but I won't give its name. At the end of the meal father asked for three large "Grand Marque" Martel brandies. Dad had an amazing nose, something I sadly have not inherited. He could smell any French wine and tell you the grape type, the year, the region, and possibly, the name of the man who picked the grapes!!

On smelling and tasting his, he asked the sommelier to bring the bottle as he was not happy with the brandy, claiming it was not what he ordered. The bottle came and another measure was poured. Still not happy father said to the sommelier, "Can I introduce you to my two guests, this is Jacques Martel and his brother Francois and I am the sole importer of Martel brandy into the UK, and that is not what the label says it is." The sommelier quietly removed all the brandy and brought over a sealed bottle, saying "This bottle is on the house, sir."!

Unfortunately, this practice is much too prevalent in our trade; only a few years ago in Crete I was served Metaxa brandy in place of Hennessey XO, my own fault, it was so cheap it could never have been Hennessey. The bar manager wouldn't have it though and begrudgingly gave me Courvoisier VSOP as a replacement, more Metaxa, of course!

Forays into the restaurant world

In 1959, having moved from Rigby and Evans and now the managing director of Seagrams UK, dad decided that he had enough of the drinks trade, so he and mum started a small restaurant and delicatessen in Knutsford, a small town in the heart of Cheshire.

They called the restaurant the "Hat and Feather" on account of a picture my father had of him and mum in which she was wearing a hat with a large pheasant feather protruding from it – as good a reason as any for naming a restaurant!

Mum, as far as I knew, had only worked during the war. She had married dad just before hostilities began, aged 19 and then spent the war years working in Blenheim Palace for MI5. She never would tell us what she did as she had "signed the Secrets Act", which meant that, even in 2002, when we visited Blenheim and she told the assembled crowd, much to their joy, and my embarrassment, about her war years there, she still didn't say exactly what she had done.

After the war she spent 15 years touring Europe, visiting wine estates in France, Spain and Germany – not such a bad life. So it was a bit of culture shock when thrown into the busy world of a small restaurant, but one, like everything mother did, she did one hundred per cent and with no complaints.

It is now 1960 and my 13 year old sister Arlette (Letty as we call her), named after the wife of a French wine shipping friend of dad's in Bordeaux, and myself, settled into this small house in the main street of Knutsford. I actually quite liked it; there was a bustle, shops and life everywhere and the golf club was within walking distance.

When we had lived in Bromborough, we had to cycle or walk quite a way to see such things and, whilst living above a restaurant was quite cramped, I didn't mind. My sister on the other

Grandpa strutting his stuff in Nice in 1917

hand, was not amused. Her life of luxury had suddenly taken a wrong turn, but she got used to it, eventually, although eventually was quite a long time!!

Mum and dad worked extremely hard and soon had three delicatessen shops. Dad took on a partner to help run the two new establishments, unfortunately the partner was dishonest and the partnership was declared bankrupt, but dad being the honourable man he was, repaid all the people they owed money to from the profits of the restaurant. I don't think mum or dad took a day off for five years. I so admire that sort of attitude.

For holidays Letty and I would stay with Granny (Grandpa having passed away) who now lived with my father's only sister, Auntie Barbie and husband Uncle Phil on their farm in Eardisland, Herefordshire in a huge pile of stones called Lynch Court.

Uncle Phil had owned a cotton factory which he sold soon after the war and bought Gliffaes Hotel situated outside Crickhowell between Brecon and Abergavenny. Sam Brabner, his manager from the factory, with Jane, his wife ran the hotel whilst Uncle Phil and Auntie Barbie ran the farm.

They had a tennis court, bowling green and croquet lawn, all of which we played before dinner and Uncle Phil was an eight handicap golfer so trips in his Bentley to Kington golf club, the highest golf club in England (it's nearly in Wales), was a regular event. It amused me that

Uncle John's Street in Rugles – Northern France

Aunt B gave her 365B Porsche to the gardener because it had developed a little rust. It had only travelled 18,000 miles.

I loved Granny Stirling. Dorothy was her Christian name and Grandpa always called her Dolly. She was a proper lady, a little removed from real life. She had always had a maid, Doris, who worked for her for 50 years.

When I discussed the student "sit ins" in 1967 – complaining about student fees and the like – Granny's response was "when we were unhappy as children, we just went round to our friends' houses and played tennis". I explained it wasn't a luxury the modern student had.

She expected us always to change into a shirt and tie for dinner – something she relaxed in her later years. I used to love her stories and only wish I had listened harder, or taped them – I would love to hear her voice again, her stories of Zeppelins flying over London in the First World War, or when aged about 14, coming back from La Baule in France by diligence (horse and trap) and reaching St Malo, to hear that Queen Victoria had died!

She would regale me with stories of her and Grandpa driving around France to meet the likes of Madame Roederer, Monsieur Martel and many other wine growers and shippers in France, Spain and Portugal.

Europe in the 1920s and 1930s was less cluttered and places like La Baule, which is now a mini Bournemouth, she would talk about the only hotel on the front – La Commercial – a far cry from today. Soon after the war she had a heart attack and Grandpa even discussed a possible funeral with the vicar. She recovered and then lived 23 years after Grandpa who died in 1962 aged 81, Granny living until she was 97. She always finished her meal with fruit salad and I can hear her saying "A little of what you fancy does you good" when a glass of wine was poured. Although she was quite deaf in her 90s, she could hear a Champagne cork being extracted, however quietly, and her comment was always "Ooo that's a nice sound.". On her 90th birthday after her sherry, red and white wine she asked for a kummel, and then another kummel – I was getting concerned and suggested maybe two was enough – to which she replied 'My dear Andrew, a bird cannot fly on one wing!' Such a great lady.

We would also stay with my mother's only sister, Auntie D at the Meade in Chew Stoke, Somerset. My mother and Auntie D's mum – Gan – would stand on the tennis court, tiny and old as she was, on the other side of the net and hit balls to me. Strange that I never took to tennis, but preferred squash! I think collecting the balls put me off. Gan, with Gampa Hunter, as we called them, lived in a cottage at the bottom of the garden – great holidays.

The final two families I would occasionally holiday with were my father's first cousin – Uncle John Stirling, wife Barbara and four girls, Libby, Jackie, Wendy and Penny. Uncle John and I would escape to the nearest golf club – we always went on holiday to Cornwall as Uncle John had a boat in St. Mawes. He played off a handicap of two and had been an Oxford Blue, so I listened hard to his advice. He was also a very large man, about 6'3" tall with a large frame, so not a man you ignored.

Uncle John and Auntie Peggy Rickman were the other family I would sometimes find myself staying with. Uncle John was my godfather and best man at mum and dad's wedding. He was the first horse racing broadcaster on TV in the early sixties and lived in Hazelmere, Surrey. They were very proper people and I was always told to be on my best behaviour when staying there. Once, at dinner, aged about 13, I was served with fried liver, something I didn't like, but to be polite I ate it and when offered more I found myself saying "Yes, please". I love liver now – years of not being able to leave the table at school or at home until you had eaten everything on your plate has stood me in good stead – I don't think there is anything I now won't eat! Years later I read a book that Uncle John had written about his life and discovered that my grandfather had been West of England Tennis champion in 1912 and captain of Stinchcombe golf club 1936 and 1937.

In 1963 I started life at Blundells School in Tiverton, my father's old school. Unfortunately because of the distance from Cheshire I never saw my parents during the term time, but hey, I quite liked school – mainly the sports. I remember in the Spring Term all the school had to participate in "The Russell" – a six-mile run through boggy countryside. Within 600 yards of the start you had to run through a large stream – The Lowman – normally in full flood, and continue for the next five and a half miles, absolutely soaked – I hardly think health and safety would allow it today!

The school had all kinds of sporting opportunities, so I developed my squash, rugby, hockey and golfing skills and played for the 1st XV. I was awarded my house cricket and squash caps and on activity afternoons I would wander around old Iron Age forts in the countryside; funny that, now at Wolfscastle, we own one!!

It was at this point that I decided to either become an archaeologist or antique collector. I had given a lecture at school about coin collecting and my own collection was growing. Back in the holidays, I helped at the family restaurant.

To start with I was only allowed to wash up, this was in a small room to the side of the kitchen. One Whit weekend when we had been particularly busy, I had been working all afternoon, washing dishes, only to be found at 10 o'clock by my parents sitting on a stool at the sink, hands in the water, fast asleep. At 11, I had joined the real world of catering!

To help promote the business, my father sponsored a donkey in the local donkey derby and I, being the smallest, was chosen to be the jockey. Having been chased out of a field by a Shetland pony at an early age, I had a serious dislike for anything horse like, so was a very tentative contender whilst sitting on the starting line.

The whistle blew and off the others went. My donkey, unfortunately performed an about-face and wandered off in the opposite direction. By the time I had it turned around all the others had finished, so it was a very lonely and red-faced 'jockey' who eventually reached the finishing line. My father was dismayed until he read the local paper the next day featuring me and my donkey on the front page – good publicity after all!

Fortunately, in 1966, all my parents' hard work paid off and the Good Food Guide rated The Hat and Feather one of the best 18 restaurants in Britain. We had expanded by buying the house next door and, boy, were we busy.

I remember one night, mum had overbooked the restaurant and I asked what we were going to do. She told me not to worry, not everyone will turn up – but, they all did! Mum's chance came when she heard a customer say "Oh, there is nothing on this menu I fancy". A flick of the hand and the menu was back on the bar. Mum said, "Well you better go and eat somewhere else, then." She turned to me and smiled!

They had a little black book and any customer who didn't behave properly or complained went in it and never could book again. One evening, a couple walked into the restaurant, the man was dressed in checked trousers, a patterned jacket, wearing every colour imaginable. I remember thinking, he's about to be ejected, but, quite to the contrary, dad asked, very politely, how could he help.

My father, spent the war years in India in charge of a battery. Having arrived in Durban, South Africa in 1939, one boat went to Singapore and spent the whole war in a Japanese prisoner of war camp, whilst my father's boat went to Calcutta where he involved himself in all aspects of Indian life. I regret I never asked him about his experiences, but I think he had a very interesting, non-dangerous war but it probably made him capable of speaking to all types of people and not to judge – a good trait to have in life.

The multi-coloured character said, "Eee are you the owner, like? Cos me and the wife know 'owt about food and wine, but would like to learn." It transpired that he was a scrap dealer from Wigan and Mateus Rose plus fish and chips were the extent of his wine and gastronomic knowledge.

Within three years, dad had taught him a lot about both food and wine and they became good friends – he, of course, had spent a lot of money with us, which helped!

The famous "Bra In My Soup" story, occurred when our Anglo Indian head chef, Mrs. Pringle had popped into town and bought a large bra (she was a large lady), wrapped in a brown bag.

She placed the bag containing the bra in the stock pot in the pot store whilst she carried on with her work. A junior had taken the pot, they are very tall pots, put it on the stove and deposited all the ingredients a stock would need; bones, onions, carrots, celery, etc along with a lot of water. Three hours later, mum stirred the pot and wondered why brown paper was floating on the top, dug deeper and out came the bra!

By mid-December 1966, I thought that maybe, catering was a possible career. My Latin and Greek being very inadequate, I decided archaeology and antique collecting were more of a hobby than a vocation.

I enjoyed food of all types; it is amazing that as a child aged ten I would only eat the plainest of cooking, but, by 16, kofta curry, chicken liver pate, jugged hare, chicken Elizabeth, lobster thermidor, and such like, I ate daily. Basically, we ate whatever had reached its sell by date. Mum and dad thought it was fine to kill the family, but not the customers.

Switzerland 'behind bars!'

I am now 17, just left the cosseted life of public school, I have a sore knee, as, unfortunately, whilst playing rugby, I twisted it and had to have a cartilage removed. It had been decided that a winter season in one of Switzerland's finest hotels would be a good starting point for a boy going into catering.

It was for this reason that I found myself on December 19th, 1966, after eighteen hours on a train, sitting on a bench at 4 o'clock in the morning in Basel Station. I was waiting for immigration to open so that I could have a medical (to show I wasn't carrying any nasty diseases) and get my passport stamped.

The temperature was about -3 degrees Celsius and I wasn't dressed for it. It was a very long, cold four hours until eventually I had the medical. Back onto another train which terminated at Lauterbrunnen.

Up the funicular railway which, eventually took me to my destination – Murren, a beautiful alpine village perched on the side of the valley in the Bernese Oberland. Looking across at the Eiger, Monk and Jungfrau Mountains, three of the highest peaks in the Alps – spectacular. The village was dominated by The Palace, which was to be my prison for the next nine months.

I say prison, because the first thing they did was take my passport and hand it to the police – there was no way of escape. I was then put to share a room with a young Tunisian who started his washing routine at 6 o'clock every morning. It lasted about an hour, and took in every orifice known to man.

Unfortunately, his feet stank – bless him, I think he was one of those people whose feet always stank, regardless of how many times he changed his socks, you could smell him long before you saw him.

My uniform was handed to me, a large striped apron, I was positioned in front of the dishwasher, where, with a couple of Portuguese, who spoke no English and argued with each other all the time, I stayed for 15 hours a day, for a month, washing dishes.

Not exactly the way I planned to spend Christmas. I wrote a letter on Christmas Day to my parents, saying how unhappy I was, to which my mother replied suggesting I came home. Dad read the letter and crossed out the come home bit and put "stick at it," and whatever dad said, you did, so I stayed.

One thing you do learn when you wash up is do not upset the guy at the bottom. One waiter called Nino, all the waiters were Italian, who was about five foot tall, with social problems, obviously didn't like the Portuguese, so they, in turn, were not friendly to him. The waiters were highly skilled at carrying a tray on their shoulders, something I learnt to do, on which was precariously balanced the main courses, side dishes and drinks.

The kitchen was some 80 yards away from the restaurant and the waiters would fly past the wash up area towards swing doors into the dining room. As Nino ran by with his full tray, one of the Portuguese deftly lifted the bottle of wine off the back of the tray. This upset the balance, the tray started to fall forwards, Nino ran faster to try to counteract it, but all too late. The whole tray ensemble smashed into the door, nothing was saved. The floor was littered with Wiener schnitzel, glass, plates, cutlery, vegetables and more, a real mess.

Now he had to go back into the kitchen and ask for the entire meal again. The kitchen brigade were all Swiss and they didn't like the Italians, so I felt sorry for Nino as he ducked out of the kitchen with everything the chef could lay his hands on being thrown at him.

After a month I moved up to floor porter – you collected bags, fetched and carried for the chambermaids, hoovered the long corridors and 12 bedrooms each day. But the first job in the morning was to gather up all the shoes that had been put outside the doors the night before and clean them.

On my first morning in post, I duly collected all the shoes, cleaned them and then the fun started. I had made no note as to which shoes belonged to whom. I placed the shoes as best as I could remember and then watched in despair as the guests padded up and down the corridor to collect their shoes. The plus side was that for the rest of the week, people were reluctant to put their shoes out, thus shrinking my workload.

I worked in most areas of the hotel, helped the maintenance man and toiled in the laundry room. One of my jobs was to sit on this huge rotary washer on its final spin as one of the bolts was coming loose and everyone was fearful it would fly off its mountings; if the added weight didn't work, a young Briton was obviously expendable! The manager's wife, who, like her husband was a lovely person, but totally in the wrong job, decided to wash a stained carpet in the washing machine. That was nearly the end of it and, of course, the carpet shrunk, so never fitted the room it came out of. They had to have a new carpet. The mood was not good in the hotel that day.

I would spend the couple of hours I had off in the afternoons listening to the Italian band practising in the hotel's nightclub, The Inferno. Everyone spoke French in the hotel, the language of catering in those days – my French was becoming tolerable, so the band asked me to explain the meaning of the words in the English songs they sang.

First of all, I had to work out the lyrics myself and then translate them into French, difficult. The first song they wanted me to tackle was "Whiter Shade Of Pale" by Procol Harum. I thought, and have for many years, that the first line was "Skip a line, bang bang go" instead of "We skipped the light fandango". It is hardly surprising that my services were not required for long!

My life improved after two months when two 25 year olds from Canada, working their way around Europe, had run out of money and were offered jobs washing-up in the hotel. They took me under their wing and I started learning about the mature things in life, chiefly I have to say women and drink! Being a 17 year old, I had little experience of such things, remember it was 1966 and I had just finished at an all-boys school!

I had become a commis waiter at this stage and during my trips in and out of the kitchen had noticed where all the keys were hidden when the chefs locked up and went home for the night. This was useful information for the two Canadians as they weren't fond of the food the staff were given by the chefs. Once, we had ox tongue casserole, I thought it was quite pleasant but Terry, the noisier of the two, asked me what he was eating, I told him "Ox tongue", "What's that?", he asked.

I made the noise of a cow and held my tongue and said tongue. He promptly threw up and didn't trust anything the chef gave him to eat again. So began the late-night skirmishes into the kitchen looking for food.

I would finish work around midnight and scuttle upstairs to see what delights the guys had managed to secrete from the kitchen. On one particular occasion, all was gloom – "What have you guys got", I asked. "Bones" was the reply. What they thought they were doing, I don't know, because they had brought the stockpot up, they said they thought it was a casserole and they were going to store it in buckets outside the window, bearing in mind it's winter in the Alps, and heat it up on the little camp burner they had.

It was of no use, the pot, bones and all, were thrown into the deep snow, not to be seen again until the thaw. Funnily enough a month or so after they arrived, they were sacked. I wasn't too happy, life became a little less interesting.

I worked at the Palace Hotel all through the summer. The Alps are equally as beautiful at that time of year – the flowers, cows with their bells and fantastic mountain backdrops. The work was hard, long days with little time off.

I was working 15-hour days, seven days a week – all the staff worked on that basis and then they would take October and November off, go back to their families in Portugal, Spain or Italy and then back for another 10 months of continual work, a tough life, but it was like being in a big family "under the stairs".

By the end I knew it was the life for me, hard work, complex, varied and in nine months I had had two years' worth of experience, and could speak passable French with some German and Italian words. So I returned home immediately and enrolled on a catering course.

Sandy Blackpool

So it was in September 1967, aged 18, I started my three-year hotel manager's course at Blackpool Catering College, Courtfield as it was known to the locals. We all dressed as hotel managers, striped "morning suit" trousers, black jacket, white shirt, black shoes, silver tie.

Everyone else in the college dressed as they wanted. After a year someone decided we should not be forced to dress accordingly so the uniform disappeared. Possibly not a wise move, as standards seemed to slip, but we, at least, blended in with the other students.

On inauguration day, I met Sandy Falconer – Alexander Wilson Falconer, to be precise, a rather geeky looking character with his large glasses and wavy blond hair. He made some comment that amused me, and I thought, I could be friends with this guy, and so I was, best friends, brothers even for the next 42 years.

He was the only son of Dr. and Dr. Falconer, although mum didn't practise, she was the receptionist in the surgery. She was a lovely, lovely lady and dad was a really caring, old-fashioned sort of doctor. I used to love my weekends at 73 Penkett Road in Wallasey, which is where Sandy lived with his three sisters, Anne, Mary and Alison.

Wallasey is only eight miles from Bromborough and Sandy had gone to a school only a mile from The Leas, my early prep school. We found we knew a lot of the same people, had probably played football and rugby against each other, and then, like I had, he followed his father's footsteps and had gone to his father's school Fettes, in Edinburgh.

For the next three years we were inseparable. We lived together in a small flat by the South Pier, partied and drank together, and played a lot of golf with another friend Simon Ashcroft. We would pretend that we were Gary Player, Arnold Palmer and Jack Nicklaus and ask each other what we were trying to do with each shot as if being interviewed by Henry Longhurst, the commentator of the day, silly days. I, of course, was Gary Player, being the shortest of the three, Sandy was Arnie!

College wasn't hard, the course was split up into some practical and some theory, the theory was law, maintenance, accountancy, French, rules and regulations relating to the industry and food hygiene.

The practical was waiting on, bar work, and cooking. Well, the practical side was a breeze as, unlike most of the students, I had a sound grounding in those areas, also, very few others had a knowledge of French – any homework I had I would do in the French lessons, leaving plenty of time for the evening "entertainment".

Restaurant Les Flots Bleu

For the first summer holiday, Sandy and I secured a job, with my father's help, in a restaurant in Royan called Les Flots Bleu on the west coast of France – a lovely seaside resort at the mouth of the Gironde estuary. We travelled from Liverpool to Bordeaux in an old tramp steamer – it was horrible – the captain was a gruff Dutchman and all his crew were Portuguese.

We were given a hold by the engine room to sleep in and spent three days feeling and being sick as the boat rolled its way down the coast, through the Bay of Biscay to Bordeaux. Boy, were we glad to reach dry land!

We booked into an old fashioned, small hotel called the "Hotel Carnot", a name I will never forget as about a year later when talking about the 10 weeks we spent in France neither Sandy nor I could remember the name of the hotel. I was woken at 3 o'clock in the morning by Sandy saying "Hotel Carnot", "Hotel Carnot" and neither of us ever forgot the name.

For the first week my father, through his business connections in the wine trade, had arranged for us to work in the cellars of Eschanauer's, a large wine producing and shipping company.

We were put to cleaning old barrels and bottling wine, and, of course, a little tasting. I could well understand why everyone who worked there seemed to have large red noses!

On our last day, all the "sons" of the people with whom Eschanauer conducted business around the world – about twelve of us – were treated to a tour of the chateaux they either owned or had connections with. This culminated in a grand meal at Ch. Rauzan Segla, a fine claret producing estate.

Waitresses with white gloves treated us to sumptuous fayre which we washed down with the best that Bordeaux could produce – a real feast – when coffee arrived it was accompanied by a Grand Marque Cognac. I remember it had 1898 on the label – God knows what that would cost today!

At this stage I had never drunk brandy, so, not wishing to seem rude, took a deep breath, and swallowed my large brandy in one. I now couldn't breathe or talk, so when the ever attentive waitress saw I had finished and I gave no reply when she asked "Encore monsieur", she refilled my glass with an even larger brandy.

This time I sipped it treating it with the respect a good cognac deserves, and slowly began to like it. Coupled with all the wine we had drunk Sandy and I staggered out into the blazing sunshine, it was a particularly hot summer, and promptly fell asleep on the bus back to

Bordeaux, a good way to finish our week.

One of the guys entertained by Eschanauer was called Howard Blum, his dad was a very well-to-do wine shipper from New York and had sent Howard to Europe to visit the chateaux where the wine he was selling in America came from. He had also given Howard a ridiculously huge weekly allowance which allowed him to go and do what he wanted.

A car, of course, was thrown into the bargain, we thought ourselves lucky when we asked if he would run us the 80 miles to Royan, and had a positive response. Lucky? Well, Howard wasn't that bothered which side of the road he drove on and, as he overtook something on a corner, he would say "You guys feel like a suicide run?" Royan could not have come soon enough! Goodbye, Howard.

Les Flots Bleu was run by a father and son. The father spent all day standing by the rubbish bin checking that we didn't throw anything away he could reuse, and the son would sit by the till taking the money and watching the women. His wife rarely came to the restaurant, which was a good thing because he was blatantly having a good time with the girl who ran the laundry. The daily routine was to rise at 9 o'clock, work to 3 o'clock, back at 6 o'clock and finish at around midnight.

It was an enjoyable experience, great camaraderie, but Sandy had a propensity for dropping things. His greatest achievement was to put 14 large dinner plates on the edge of a small table, he then turned to adjust something on the guest's table and was too late to stop all the plates from falling off and hurtling across the tiled floor, covering the full length of the restaurant.

It seemed to take an eternity until the plates had finished their journey. The noise was deafening, every plate had smashed and you could now have heard a pin drop, not one of the 100 or so diners uttered a word! Not surprisingly, when, ten weeks later, we were paid, Sandy received a little less than I did. "Pour les assiettes," Sandy was told.

Like a few of the other waiters, we didn't have work permits, which meant when the inspectors came to check on the restaurant, we had to run across the road to the beach and wait until they left – the poor customers couldn't understand why suddenly the service deteriorated in the middle of the meal.

Two summers later, when we returned, the restaurant had closed, it was a shame, as the food was very good – I remember they made an excellent "mouclade," a delicious alternative to moules mariniere and their pâté de campagne was to die for.

The piece de resistance was a "Barque de fruits de mer", a large wicker boat festooned with seaweed with a sample of just about everything that had a shell on it and came from the sea.

We returned back to college at the end of the summer to another term of golf and parties, Blackpool was not a bad place to be for a young person; plenty of clubs and bars.

In my first year I had bought a 1947 Armstrong Siddely Hurricane Coupe, not a sensible car like a mini or A40 that the others who could afford cars had. I preferred interesting motors.

I paid £32 for it and sold it 12 months later for £16. It cost me a fortune to keep on the road as I used to drive it flat out down the motorway – about 80mph – with the result that the big ends went – twice – very expensive. The M6, in those days, had very few cars on it, it's more like a car park now; how things have changed.

My favourite restaurant of the late 60s, where I would entertain girlfriends, was the Leigh Arms in Prestbury. The first time I ate there, whilst I did have a jacket on I didn't have a tie, so one was offered to me and I didn't forget again.

I always had the same meal, so boring – Coquilles St Jacques and Tournedos Rossini – we never cook such things now as the modern chef frowns on such dishes, but I bet there is a market for them. I will have these dishes for my 70th birthday – if I get there!

For my next holiday job I travelled down to Salcombe in Devon to work in a small hotel called The Sun. It was not the most salubrious of establishments; the chef would collect up everything that was left after breakfast, add some stock, liquidise it and then serve it as soup for the evening. Quite cost effective, but not something I would recommend.

A girl from college, whom I was quite fond of came with me, which lightened the job a little, but I don't think the experience of the hotel did a lot for my career.

One more year at Blackpool Catering College and then freedom. Sandy and I both passed, it was pretty hard not to, in fact, 50 of us had started the course and 36 of us finished it. I think the 14 that gave up just couldn't take the boredom. I just wanted the diploma in the hope that it would help my career. All in all, I had had a pretty good time and Sandy and I decided to take my little Austin Healey Sprite and spend the summer camping our way around France.

I loved the country and still do. I love the language, so expressive and beautiful to listen to. I can spend days walking around the markets, the smell of the cheeses, sampling the wines, tasting the meats and pates.

We drove around Brittany staying in campsites, cruising the beaches and the bars – my only real memory of the first three weeks was that of water dripping through the tent which was an old one of my father's from the war, which old age had made porous.

Still, copious amounts of wine, French bread sticks, laden with pate de campagne and French cheese allayed our discomfort. Eventually we arrived at Royan, we had decided to revisit the friends we had made and the places we had come to know. We picked up a couple of French students, which improved our French, greatly, as neither spoke any English.

We sunbathed on the long, sandy beach by day, went round the bars at night ending up at the casino or the "Club Pirate" where we danced the night away – oh to be young and carefree again!

Cymru am Byth!

A telegram arrived from my father in mid-September 1970, saying "have bought small hotel in St. David's called St Non's, do you and Sandy want to come and run it?" My mum and dad, after 11 years, had decided to sell the Hat and Feather and move to Wales. Sandy and I had not decided what else to do, we were still in holiday mode, so, why not. We drove back to Britain for what we thought would be about two years, to get the hotel up and running as it would look good on our curriculum vitae, and then move on.

What we found was a 12-bedroom hotel built by a character called Trevor Jones, who had, obviously taken a few short cuts; the corridors slightly sloped – "a gentle incline", as he put it. When later on we added an extension, we found the plans only bore a cursory resemblance to what was actually built.

Sandy and I were 21 when we embarked on this enterprise and whilst we were both keen and had experience of hotel and restaurant work, running your own place was very different.

Father was there to help, but he and mother spent April to September in Minorca, where they had bought a small villa, so during the busy months, Sandy and I were left to cope on our own.

Gianni Baptiste di Lorenzo, my father's head waiter from Knutsford came down to help us. He was excellent and I have not met many people who could wait on as well as him.

He went on to run his own establishments and is still in St. David's to this day. I remember our first chef was a lady called Sally Newton, quite a large girl, with a matching personality – but she could cook. I would run the kitchen on the two days she had off. We soon made a name for ourselves with our bar buffet lunches and creative dishes.

We had a public bar that attracted locals and holidaymakers alike, I suppose we were very naïve and, of course, English, so fair game for the locals.

We were told that a typical Welsh greeting was "Iechyd da pob Cymro twll dyn pob Sais" which roughly means "cheers to all the Welsh, up the backsides of the English" but perhaps not quite so politely!

Dai Sparks, the local electrician, and good friend, told us what it meant before we had insulted too many people. In fact, they were all friendly, just having a bit of a laugh at our expense.

Quite a few of them spent a lot of time with us, to the detriment of their marriages, I suspect. One particular character, Byron, when having consumed his usual 14 pints or so, sung with a lovely tenor voice. We were privileged to hear some superb singing in the bar after the amber nectar started flowing.

On one occasion Byron jumped into his Triumph Herald, well, having located it, crawled in, I suspect, set off down the slope in front of the Bishop's Palace, taking a sharp left towards Porth Clwys. Unfortunately, he hadn't shut his door properly and as he took the left turn, fell out of his car and was deposited on the road watching his car glide into the wall. Five minutes later he was back in the bar for another pint! Thankfully we have come a long way in clamping down on drink driving since those days.

Another story attributed to Byron was, when walking home, he tried to light his pipe, but the wind was too strong so he turned into the wind and, after a short time, managed to get his pipe lit, forgetting he had turned round, he continued his walk and ended up back where he started!

A couple of stories I remember are, firstly the fire. At around 8 o'clock water started dripping into the bar, so I ran upstairs into the attic room where Sandy and I slept, only to see flames in the roof. Fortunately a slate had fallen into the room and severed a water pipe that was successfully spraying the flames and thus controlling the fire.

I ran downstairs and rang the fire brigade. We were in the middle of serving a retirement dinner for some 60 guests so I quietly announced to them that there was a fire but everything was under control. This announcement was greeted with hoots of laughter as the assembled crowd thought I was joking. It was the retirement of the local fire chief, what are the odds of that! PC Morris located himself at the bottom of the stairs and after his third whisky that I had given him, announced that it was the best fire he had ever been too. The fire brigade soon quelled the flames and normality was resumed.

I stayed at St. Non's for five years and in that time we built another seven bedrooms, added another bar and extended both the restaurant and kitchen. People would book from one year to the next creating a regular holidaying clientele and Brawdy, the R.A.F. station and American Marine base, was in full flow and a good source of trade for us.

The three loves of my life were good food, fast cars and squash, well, there is a fourth, but we'll leave that one out. The first one, good food, was something we tried to create daily and we ate out in all the local restaurants of the day.

Two favourites in the early 70s were the Pantry in Newport and Chez Gilbert in Haverfordwest; both long gone now.

Robin Evans, who ran the Pantry, came into the bar one day with the great late Keith Floyd. The original food presenter, as they had both been friends in Bristol. What a great character he was, I enjoyed that afternoon raconteuring as my family had come from Bristol and Keith had just sold his last restaurant there. My cousin Wendy had worked for him and like his TV programmes, much hilarity was the norm.

As for cars, I had sold my Sprite for an Alfa Romeo G.T.V, a beautiful car, but unreliable, then I had a TR4A and, in 1973, with some money my granny gave me, I bought a new TR6.

For its day, it was quite quick and, being a soft top, I loved the summers; oh to have the summer of 1976 back again!

The Wolfscastle Wallbangers

My favourite sport is squash, but since I had come to St. David's, I had found nowhere and no one to play with.

I started playing squash at the tender age of 10 at my prep school and continued to do so throughout public school and college, running the team at Blackpool when we played the colleges and universities in the area.

My regular sparring partner was James Grimke Drayton, he was the Cheshire junior champion and very useful. We played three times a week, great fun.

The only court close to St Non's was in a hangar at Brawdy and you had to be invited to play there. My chance came when a young Canadian called Eric was talking in the bar, lauding what titles he had won at squash. I went over with a £5 note and laid down a challenge, in the hope that he was bragging a little. He invited me up for a game, but he wasn't. I could get close enough for him to invite me regularly to Brawdy for games and I met a couple of rather useful RAF pilots as well – so my love of squash was reignited.

One of these characters was a gentleman called Peter Cross. Peter was a helicopter man and good squash player, he became my regular sparring partner from 1974 to 1979. He nearly always won, being 25 years my senior, I felt obliged to let him.

In his posh English voice, when I asked for a let in the hope of being awarded a stroke, he would decline it and say, "My dear boy I'll tell you when it's a let", but he was a very canny player and I enjoyed many, many games with him. We would then retire to the bar for copious amounts of red biddy – as he called wine.

His lovely daughter, Affra, came to work in the kitchen in my early years in Wolfscastle. She sounded a bit like the Queen in 1953, quite 'far back' as they say, but the locals embraced her and as Peter would have said, she was a "great gal!"

The only other sport I would play was golf – Sandy and I would creep off to St David's Golf Club either before breakfast or after lunch and play a quick nine holes. I rarely play competitions but I won the St David's open, sometime in the 80s scoring a 78 on a very windy day. I scored the second lowest gross, my handicap being 13, meant I won quite easily. I hardly play at all now, sadly, but when Ollie and Robbie are old enough, no doubt I'll be dusted down and dragged back onto the course.

For a couple of years Simon Hopkinson, who has recently had a television programme and written some excellent cookery books, helped run the kitchen. He was and is a real talent and thanks to him I never put a sharp knife in the sink. He gave me a real telling off for doing so – quite rightly, as you can easily cut yourself when groping around under the soap suds.

I had bought a golden Labrador called Mutley – as dogs did in those days, he would wander around St David's causing a degree of havoc. Sergeant Davies (Trevor) – one of the nicest policemen you would ever want to meet, would call in and ask me to collect Mutley from a campsite as he had emptied a tent whilst the owners were out – or could you meet the bus from Solva as your dog is on it!

The amount of single wellingtons Mutley collected from people's front doors was frightening. When I bought a home in Treffgarne, he would collect the milk left by the milk lady, Daphne Lewis; I found at least 50 empty milk bottles in some waste ground at the top of our garden!

In 1976, I was invited to go to Kent to play squash by David Morris, a farmer from Angle, South Pembrokeshire, he wasn't built for speed, but was one of the sweetest strikers of a squash ball I have ever played against, and the best player in the county at the time. Along with his brother-in-law, Rod Thomas, an estate agent, and a couple of other guys, we found ourselves in Kent playing against virtually the Kent County team.

The only game we won was the drinking game – a very wet weekend as I remember, but, during which I decided I wanted to find a house and build two squash courts alongside it and run it as a squash club and restaurant with rooms.

I know let's buy a hotel!

Rod was on the phone the following morning suggesting that Allt yr Afon might be an option as it was for sale for £35,000. It had two lounges, a large dining room, kitchen, seven bedrooms and two bathrooms and was once a vicarage owned by the Tucker-Edwardes family of the nearby Sealyham mansion.

After a visit, I decided it would be a perfect property so persuaded my father and cousin Sally to invest, along with £7k I had saved myself. This left a shortfall of £14k, so off I went to the Midland Bank, Mr. Thomas was the manager – to ask for funding.

A forecast was created, costs of the building project, and, in the end, I needed around £40k, a lot of money at the time. Mr. Thomas said he would have to get agreement from head office, so come back in a week or so. A few days later, Rod Thomas informed me that he had another buyer so if I didn't put down a deposit it would be gone. Quickly I rang Mr. Thomas who said "Go on then, buy it, I'm sure head office will say "yes", so the deal was struck. The following week I met up with Mr. Thomas and asked if head office had given the go-ahead – to which he told me they had said No! "What do we do now", I asked. "Don't worry", he said, "I told them it was too late". Hallelujah, if only all bank managers were like that!

By May 1977 the hotel, which I renamed the Wolfscastle Country Hotel was open. I had brought the head chef from St. Non's with me – Rosanna Lloyd, a very proper young lady, daughter of a solicitor from Monmouth and a fine cook, and with Affra helping as second chef we soon gained a good reputation for our innovative food which featured in the Good Food Guide and by 1978 the squash courts were completed.

Rosie, as we called her, worked with me for about four years and decided that coupled with the four years she had worked with me in St Non's it was time to move on. She applied for a job in "The Lady" magazine, working as a chef to a person of note! She got the job and found

Wolfscastle Country Hotel and Restaurant

Wolfscastle, Nr. Haverfordwest, Pembrokeshire.
Telephone: Treffgarne 225

T4 C4 31·8·44

	£	p
2 Melon	1	30
2 Soup	1	10
2 Salmon	6	30
1 Veal	3	30
1 Steak	3	40
4 Sweet	2	60
4 Coffee	1	00
Drinks		55
1 carafe wine	2	20

VAT No. 124-9186-63

No. 1733

	21	80
	19	55
8% VAT	1	56
Total	21	11
	23	54

One of our very first bills (1978ish). Note the V.A.T at 8%, dessert at 65p and coffee at 25p! Happy days!

herself at Highgrove as the first chef to Prince Charles and Princess Diana. She says little of her time there, but I know she held them in high regard.

In the early years the Good Food and Egon Ronay Guide were the two books we aspired to be in and I remember in 1979, I had four single guests staying in the hotel.

Rather than have them sit on four tables I laid up a large round table and put the four of them on it. I remember the names of two of the chaps – Graham Ager and Merv Key – both frequent visitors, friends even. Of the other two, one was pretty regular, but the fourth I had never met before.

Fawlty Towers was a programme we hoteliers watched avidly and so it was that I had put down the other three main courses and was holding a duck for the gentlemen whom I had never met. So, I said "Who's having the um, um" to which he says "duck" at which point I ducked down doing a Basil Fawlty impression. The three regulars saw the funny side and laughed, but the gentleman having the duck was not amused.

I recovered quickly, apologised, and made sure I was totally professional from that moment on. On leaving the following morning he asked to see me and gave me his card, and, of course, he was the Egon Ronay inspector!

He told me that for one minute I was out of the Guide but had been reinstated because I had served him properly afterwards – you never know who you may be serving, a lesson I learnt quickly. No more Basil Fawlty impressions for me!

Meanwhile, the squash club was proving to be a huge success. We had over 200 members, ran five teams and a ladies team and you had to book at least ten days in advance for a court at a prime time.

This was due in some part to my enthusiasm for the game. When not working, I was coaching or playing guests or passing squash players. Several times I played against David Gotto, the Irish No 1 who would be going to tournaments in England; whilst it was hardly a game for him, I had a real workout.

When I had been at St Non's I had employed people without checking them out, therefore from time to time ended up with someone that maybe I should have not taken on in the first place.

I remember employing a young girl called Merna – I asked her to clear a table whilst I collected the main course – when I returned to the restaurant, a couple of startled guests were watching Merna folding up their tablecloth, having removed everything from the table!

So I was wary when a local man arrived at the front door asking me what I intended to do with the grounds – he seemed a very nice old gent, so I took him around the grounds and explained what I was thinking. After 20 minutes he said "Dei, Dei, there is a lot to do – I only need 50p an hour and will be here first thing in the morning. Thank you sir."

So, without even advertising or mentioning a job opportunity, I had secured a gardener. His name was Jim, Jim Harold Davies. Known as Jim Harold or Jim the Cider on account of the amount of cider he used to drink when working as a linesman on the railway.

At 62, the doctor had told him if he continued drinking so much cider he would only last until he was 64 – if he stopped drinking he could make 67. Jim thought about this, stopped drinking cider and drank Guinness instead – 18 pints a day to be precise, and died of a heart

Rosie and Simon Hopkinson win us an award in 1972 at the St Non's Hotel

attack aged 74 carrying home 12 bottles of Guinness. I am sure he would have been happy with that!

What a lovely character; he would sit in the corner of the bar with William John Lewis, another character (known as Will Jack), sometimes joined by the local headmaster, Brian Jones – where banter expounded – great times.

Whenever a regular diner such as Pat and Anthony Bowen, possibly my best customers over the first three decades, eating with us at least twice a week, came in, a Guinness would be bought and Jim would rise, doff his cap and say "Thank you Mr. Bowen, Sir," knowing that other customers would follow suit.

I don't think he ever, in eight years, paid for a Guinness – he was either bought them and instead of 50p an hour I gave him bottles of the stuff – I'm sure he died happy, and Dudley, my second golden Labrador, son of Mutley, and he were inseparable. Dudley died two weeks after Jim, of a broken heart, I suspect.

For the following eight years life in the hotel centred around a lot of hard work, late nights and squash. We developed a touring squash team and a character called Ian Cannell and myself started being coached by Hadyn Davies – he was in his seventies, but, in his day had been one of the best players in Britain.

He helped us to develop our games and Ian and I used to travel to tournaments around

Mr. Andrew Stirling, owner of the Wolfscastle Hotel, near Haverfordwest, with his chef, Miss Rosanna

Egon Ronay newcomer finds success is a family affair

SUCCESS IS a family affair for Mrs. Mary Baverstock, whose Merthyr hotel has won a coveted entry in the 1979 Egon Ronay good food guide published today.

For while Mrs. Baverstock helps out in the kitchen with daughter Julia, husband John is

gives the hotel a 60 per cent, rating, which takes it into the second grade class.

The Wolfscastle Hotel's restaurant is also given a mention in the guide.

Mr. Andrew Sterling, the 29-year-old bachelor owner, is delighted with the entry.

Cardiff—again Wales's top is upgraded by three per cent per cent., and the Llwynderw Abergwesyn, Powys, gets a cent. rating.

The guide commends 41 restaurants and three get th Ronay culinary star—the Sw

Rosie and I entering the Egon Ronay guide

Wales. My best result was to get to the last sixteen of the Welsh Closed where I met the then Welsh No. 1 Teifian Salisbury, game over!

Once, when playing against Conway, whilst travelling back in Ian's Ford Cortina, with his windsurfer on the roof rack, two friends Andrew John and Charles Goldsworthy, climbed out of the back windows of the car, travelling at 60mph on a main road and sat on the surfboard!

Ian slowly stopped and 'politely' asked them to come back into the car. "You're only jealous" says Andrew, "because I bet you have never done 60mph on a windsurfer!" I could write a book about our away trips and Andrew would be mentioned in most of them – quite a character!

One problem we had in the hotel was if you had guests eating in the restaurant it really didn't mix too well with raucous squash players. I put fire doors along the passageway to quell the noise.

One pair of regular players – David Llewellin, the then British Rally Champion and David Perkins, a local farmer had a tendency to get upset with themselves and each other and would proceed to smash their rackets against the walls, usually resulting in broken rackets

After a game and a few drinks, they were once seen in the car park jumping up and down on their car, only a cheap Hillman or something, until it was nearly flat. I remember telling guests as they arrived, looking a bit aghast, that it was a charity stunt!

In 1982, I married my first wife, unfortunately that didn't last and we eventually both decided enough was enough. You always blame the other one in a divorce, but, probably like most disputes, there is fault on both sides, but we had had two lovely boys, Tom and Ben, whom I am very proud of.

As I write this book, Tom is married to Jen, lives near Cardiff, and has a gorgeous little girl called Ava – just two years old – and quite recently had a boy - Henry. Ben is living the high life in London, doing a job involving computers. A subject not close to my heart – I love what you can see and discover on them but not the fact that my youngsters seem to get addicted to them.

At around this point in my life, I met Hilary and Peter Rice. Hilary came to work for us on the management team and Peter used to bring a group of characters for "squash weekends" from London, where he was working. Hilary and Peter became an item and Peter then stayed in the hotel for several months and eventually they were married. Peter was a Welsh squash international, being captain for a short period, so I had an excellent, live in, squash partner.

I remember reaching the semi-final of the county tournament one year and Peter had come along to advise me – I was playing the No. 1 seed, Simon Batten and after losing the first game 9-6, Peter gave me some advice, I then lost the second game 9-6 and this time as he came to the door of the court the only advice I got was "just enjoy it". He could see I wasn't good enough to win and he was right – I didn't!

Andrew John and I decided to buy a boat and moor it on the Cleddau estuary near Neyland, Pembrokeshire.

We only had limited funds, so for the princely sum of £450 we purchased, from a real Irish character, in Pembroke Dock, a 27-foot narrow, twin-masted, clinker-built 1952 whaler. We both fell in love with it, and so began the trips from Dale to Cresswell Quay – stopping of course at all the pubs on the river – and there are quite a few!

I remember once we read the tide table wrong and were stranded in the Griffin Inn at Dale for the whole afternoon – we got back to our moorings at 10 o'clock that night! Eventually, perhaps because we didn't paint it, it sunk at its moorings, or, as Andrew put it, "it's just a new form of fishing; you send the boat down to get them" – but, we did sell it and it was seen for some time at Porthgain, the property of Pembrokeshire's fine artist John Knapp-Fisher, now, unfortunately like the boat, sadly deceased.

Tom and Ben at the wedding

My dear friend, Sandy Falconer

David's place

It would not be fair to continue writing this book without giving a paragraph to my sister, Letty. With her husband, David, in 1975, they started their restaurant in Knutsford called David's Place, only a hundred yards from the Hat and Feather. They ran it for 30 years, moving premises to within 20 yards of the Hat and Feather until David sadly died of cancer.

Their food was excellent and the restaurant was frequented by the great and good of east Cheshire which of course involved a lot of Manchester United players. David had developed into a large "mine host" and was often seen embracing his customers a little too energetically – nearly cracking their ribs – but all of his customers were sure of a very warm welcome.

When David died, I think Letty slightly lost heart in the restaurant and sold up – married a lovely guy called John Whitehouse – who lived five houses up the road from where she lived and after 15 years, they are still happily married.

Letty has two sons, my nephews – James and William. James lives in Cheltenham and has two children, Jasmine and Edward, whilst Will lives in the south of France with his wife Sinead and two boys Magnus and Lochlyn.

They both call me "Unc" which I find amusing as they are both considerably taller and larger than me! Great characters, not exactly quiet and retiring but then David was their dad!

Annoyingly, Letty took up golf and has become very good at it and now beats me! For someone who has played all his life to be beaten by his sister, who took up the sport in her fifties, is very annoying, but, hey, it's only a game!

In the 1980s life was very hectic, building up a business and playing squash when not working. Some of the club members would stay on until very late. I remember Andrew John walking home (seven miles to Haverfordwest) one night at about 1 o'clock in the morning, as he was too drunk to drive, only to return at 4am as he had left his house keys in his car – a pint of water was consumed and he then proceeded to drive home!

Adrian Davies, who eventually headed the Pembrokeshire team that the hotel sponsored, came into my life at this time. As a young 16-year-old he was off to represent Wales in Australia and was looking for funds from all the Welsh Squash Clubs. We, as a club, collected about eighty per cent of the money he received, a fact he has never forgotten. I have asked him for so many favours since and he has never refused.

Adrian eventually became the World No. 3 squash player and, probably, one of the best of all time. When he beat the World No. 1, Chris Ditmar, to win the Dutch Open, I remember asking him where he most enjoyed playing squash – he said "Holland, because I've never been beaten there!" Another person whom I did a favour for and has never forgotten is Julian Noot, whom, with his father, Chris, owns Newport Golf Club. He coached my two older boys, who now look very adept at golf and has started to coach my two youngsters – many thanks to both these guys.

Roger Burns, my regular squash partner, myself and Barclay Guy who used to play the piano in our restaurant – great character!'

Whilst mentioning people who for several years were a real influence on the hotel I could not forget Sarah Keogh and Mary Rowlands. Sarah, as a young Irish girl, worked very hard in helping me build up the business, she in later years, was the manager and became a very capable squash player.

Sarah was a real character. Fondly remembered by many guests whom she would entertain with her Irish wit! Mary was one of those motherly people whom you instantly warmed to. She applied for the job as receptionist in about 1984 and worked for over twenty years with us. I remember Adrian Davies ringing up Mary to tell her that he had been speaking to me and that the JCBs and Drots were arriving the next day to dig up the tennis court for the underground sports hall – a £3 million pound project. It was a very flustered and worried Mary when she asked me what was going on – I guessed the culprit.

Mary's finest hour was when I was asked by a customer looking at our menu what an "Eric" was. I had played, to our chef, Steve, the Monty Python sketch where John Cleese is trying to get a license for his pet halibut called Eric. Steve had then written, instead of filet of halibut, filet of Eric, which Mary duly typed. The next day I questioned Mary as to if she had ever heard of a fish called "an Eric" to which she replied "Well, you can get a John Dory!" – Good point!

I won the combined Pembrokeshire, Carmarthenshire and Cardiganshire Over 35 Squash Tournament three times, the last time being in 1987. Consequently in 1989 I was asked to

Wolfscastle Country Hotel and Restaurant

Wolfscastle, Nr. Haverfordwest, Pembrokeshire. Telephone: Treffgarne 225

2nd August, 1979

Russell Brookes, Esq., *Paid with thanks*
The Forge House,
Inkberrow, Worcs. *Russell Brook*

Dear Russell, *6th September 2015*

    I am sorry I wasn't around when you paid
your bill and you are quite right - I should have
given you a reduction due to the fact that the
wine was not quite what you ordered.

    I suggest, therefore, that the next time you
come to stay, I will offer you a 1970 Beaune
Premier Cru "on me" by way of an anniversary
present which I should have done something about
anyway.

    Many thanks again for coming to stay with
us and I hope you had a good journey home towing
the ~~bugger~~ lugger.

              Kindest regards,

                       Andrew Stirling

**1977 & 1985 Rally Champion Russell Brookes,
eventually claimed his wine 36 years later!**

join the Cardiff Dragons – a group of touring squash players whose criteria was firstly, you
could play squash and secondly, you could socialize without making a fool of yourself. I had
many enjoyable trips with this bunch, making some very good friends.

We travelled to Amsterdam, Edinburgh, Dublin, Zurich, Berlin, Vienna, and Antibes and each trip was truly memorable – such a laugh, we were so well treated by the hosts, but too often they thought we were a serious bunch of squash players rather than a social group, and the competition was of a very high standard.

In 1990, I had a shock. I was diagnosed with cancer – low-grade non-Hodgkin's lymphoma, to be precise. In hindsight, many years of burning the candle at both ends, was probably the cause. I very quickly decided that, rather than accept chemotherapy as the only cure, I would explore complementary therapies. I read a book by a Dr. Bernie Siegl, "Love, Medicine + Miracles", himself an oncologist, who couldn't explain whilst treating patients in exactly the same way, only some would improve.

He began to realize that those that helped themselves had a much better chance of survival. I became a vegetarian, but occasionally ate deep sea fish, drank only distilled water, did visualisation, relaxation, healing, herbalism and had acupuncture.

My healer was a practitioner by the name of Thomas, who still practises, and whom I feel I owe a great debt to. Even if you think this is a load of mumbo jumbo, it does make you feel that you are making a choice and not just taking strong medicine prescribed by an overworked doctor! Anyway, after two years, a disease that I was told was incurable seemed to have left me and twenty seven years down the line I am still here – I rest my case!

In the early 80s we were invited to become members of Welsh Rarebits by the then owner and founder, Mr. Emyr Griffiths, a real Welsh character and one I have spent many happy hours with. Emyr was the marketing director of the Welsh Tourist Board and decided to "go it alone" and developed a collection of Welsh hoteliers, whose hotels, he felt, went that little bit further in offering both quality food and a warm, Welsh, welcome.

He also played golf for Wales as a junior, and was the Welsh junior champion, so golf trips were organised around Wales and England, again, some great occasions were had. Emyr does not shy away from a social and, thanks to him, we have now joined Great Inns of Britain – perhaps I should get my clubs cleaned up!

The Welsh Rarebit trips would involve other hoteliers such as Steve Hindmarsh from the Bear in Crickhowell, Robert Hughes from Penhelig Arms in Aberdovey and Meic Williams, the manager of Portmeirion – all good golfers and great guys.

Banquets "R" Us

In 1985, we built a function suite at Wolfscastle that we have now recently extended and revamped. It meant the loss of the tennis court and our energies toward squash began to wane as we found we needed more bedrooms.

So one court was forfeited, the other went the same way a few years later. At about this time, the late 80s – early 90s, we met up with the London House Band. This was a group of musicians who played with various other bands and who periodically met up to play at the

David's Place. My sister's restaurant in Knutsford

Mandy and I in 2000

My sister and I in Cardigain, 1965

Jim Harold Davies with Mutley

Andrew Stirling, with the hotel's head chef Steven Brown and 2nd chef Alexandra George with some country fayre.

Residents Bar

The hotel residents bar with its welcoming atmosphere, is where orders are taken for our à la carte restaurant and bar meals are served. Over the past 20 years we have built up an enviable reputation with our use of fresh local produce, caringly handled by our four chefs who have all been with us for 10 years or more!

The restaurant offers a professional service in a relaxed, convivial atmosphere. The hotel features in many guides and is one of only thirty or so establishments selected for inclusion in 'Welsh Rarebit Hotels: The Welsh Gold Collection.'

The Four Poster Bedroom

All our bedrooms have recently been tastefully refurbished. They have private bathrooms with showers, telephones, colour T.V. and tea or coffee facilities. The hotel is a careful blend of the old and the new, and we have tried to make all our rooms practical as well as comfortable. In total there are 20 bedrooms comprising of 5 twin, 3 singles, 2 family and 10 double rooms, nine of which are in the old house and eleven in the new wing.

The Restaurant

COUNTRY HOTEL
WOLFSCASTLE
& RESTAURANT

Welcome • Croeso

Once an old vicarage, the hotel was bought in 1976 by Andrew Stirling, and is now run by Andrew and his wife Pauline - with help over the past 10 years from Sarah Keogh and Mary Rowlands. We are very much a family affair, a fact reflected in the ambience and character of 'Allt yr Afon' (Wood by the River). Many locals still know us by this, the original name.

The Banqueting Suite

Andrew, Steve Brown and Alex George – collectively 100 years at Wolfscastle

Dover Street Wine Bar in London.

What a competent collection of players they were – Max Brittain, the resident music teacher at Eton, would craft the music and play the guitar with the help of Roger Richards on piano and Nigel Williams on drums – both in Val Doonican's band.

Clive Pracey, percussion, Malcolm Everson, wind instruments, Mike Summerland, bass guitar and Mel Collins on saxophone (who played with the Rolling Stones and Mark Knopfler). They were such an entertaining crowd of guys and they were joined by either Jenny, an awesome, characterful singer, Jackie, Young Jazz Musician of the Year or Georgie Fame, the nights were a sell-out and you were very lucky to be part of them, continuing until breakfast, at the bar on most occasions. Viv Morgan, whom himself had been Pembrokeshire's answer to Lionel Richie, Mick Jagger and others, was asked to join the band with his guitar and, being the talent he is, did not disappoint. Great, Great nights.

The function room has been host to many events and lots of weddings. I love weddings, partly because they are such joyous occasions. I say to every bride that it is the only event we get to do once, so we have to get it right. I also feel a good wedding day helps, in a small way, a marriage, so is a very important occasion.

One story I remember was of a groom searching the wedding room the following morning. I asked him what he was looking for, he replied, 'Granny'. I assured him that there were no guests left behind – 'Oh', he said, 'she died a couple of years ago and is now in an urn', we managed to find her!

Jonathan Davies and Adrian Davies. Two sporting giants.

We hosted a wedding once for a Cardigan family which involved two brothers, Paul and Tim Ringer – Paul of Wales rugby international fame and Tim, whom I often played squash against.

At about 5 o'clock I the morning, about 12 of the immediate family were crowded around the bar as Paul, who knew the words of so many pop songs of the 60s or 70s, was acting as the band leader. He decided to lean against the drawn curtains to the side of the bar, whilst smoking a large cigar, only to disappear out through the curtains onto the patio, as the double doors were open, just like in the episode of "Only Fools and Horses." I couldn't get out from behind the bar to see if he was all right as the family were incapable with laughter and leaning on the counter. Back in came Paul with a squashed cigar and looking a little shaken.

I have a huge love of classic cars as I have said, the first car I had was a 1947 Armstrong Siddely Hurricane Coupe, I then quickly followed it with a 'frog eye' and Mk1 Austin Healey Sprites, both having side screens which you unbolted when the roof was off – then the TR4A, Alfa Romeo GTV, TR6 and then my favourite car of all time, an Aston Martin DB6 Vantage. I bought it for £5k in 1978 and sold it for £23k in 1988, the exact car was for sale in Classic Car recently for £155k!

From 1988 to the present day, I have owned a couple of Jaguar XJSs, P.6 3500S Rover and SDI

3500S Rover and various BMWs, always old and usually with the three litre engine.

Thankfully, as old cars tend to break down and rust I met a local character called John Curran, an absolute genius when it comes down to cars, he has rebuilt cars for me that any other mechanic would have scrapped – and, the good news is, that with his wife Stella and daughter Belle, they now live next door to us.

Stella, a superb cake maker and Belle is best friend to my two little boys. My present 530D estate is 17 years old and I love it! I am sure my interest was brought about when travelling in my uncle's Bentley and Jensen CV8 and Grandpa's large MK VIII and IX Saloon Jags. Sometime in the late 80s I was persuaded by a good friend of mine, Malcolm Thomas, the 'mad potter' as we called him, in Simpson's Cross – to join another character called Barry Caulfield Giles and build a Motor Museum in Simpson's Cross.

I couldn't resist the chance and put £20K towards it and off went Barry to get the planning permission and start construction. When nearly completed, we realized that Barry had only got planning permission for a museum and not the café restaurant and shop that he had included, also he had built it 12 feet nearer to the road and we had a considerable overspend.

Malcolm and I had busily been talking to Lord Montague's car museum and various other characters and had managed to fill the museum, but, of course, it was inevitable that it wouldn't survive, so the bank repossessed it, all the cars went back and I was £20k worse off.

You would think this experience would put me off partnerships, far from it, a few years later, with two other guys, we bought the Kings Function Centre in Milford Haven, suffice to say, that hit all sorts of obstacles including staff pilferage, so we sold it to developers and again I was relieved of some money – not as much this time, however.

In 1994 my dad died, he was 83. I suppose not a bad age, unless, of course, you are 83! But one thing I never heard him mention was death. I, unfortunately, know or knew several people who have died younger than myself, so often think about my own funeral. I joke about the words I want to hear – "Hang on a minute, I think I saw the lid move" and then I want someone to put a little motor in the coffin that, at the press of a button, makes the lid move and a finger pops out!

At every funeral I go to now, I think of what songs I want sung – what I would like people to say and what I want on my headstone. My dad never discussed any of this, but I think my mum did well. She decided, as he liked Shakespeare, to put in the cremation book, the Bard's quote from Hamlet "to die, to sleep, to sleep perchance to dream..." and I think I would like that, it sounds very peaceful.

Moving on from morbid matters! In the late 1990s, my then wife and I got divorced – not something I would ever recommend unless there is absolutely no hope of reconciliation. For me, I suddenly felt very alone and a failure, but I knew my ex and I could not just go on sniping at each other and separation was the only choice.

When Andy met Mandy

Little did I know when I recruited Mandy Harries, a local farmer's daughter, to work at the hotel many years ago, how much a big part in my life she would later play!

I had always got on well with Mandy, but she had left Pembrokeshire and was now a teacher in Oxford.

In early 2000 and recently divorced, I gave it a chance and asked her if she would go out for dinner with me and was surprised and very pleased to receive a favourable response. Although we did decide after a year or so that the age difference was too great, so we split. But after a lot of emotional telephone calls, we went back together!

It nearly all came to an end, when, in October of 2000, whilst driving home from a lovely lunch with Mandy in Cardiff, a girl coming in the opposite direction, fell asleep at the wheel and drove head on into me! When I came to, I was upside down in the hedge and my feet were trapped by the pedals, other than that I thought I was fine.

Stopping abruptly at a combined speed of 120 mph doesn't do your internal organs any favours and the ambulance and fire crew were cutting the roof of my car off to get me to hospital as fast as possible. Apparently, if they had been another five minutes later, I would have died as I was bleeding internally from a ruptured bowel and by the time I was on the operating table, I had lost a considerable amount of blood.

Thanks to the skills of a Dr. Jaffery, the offending bowel was cut out, about four feet of it in all and after a four-hour operation, I was sewn back up.

Thankfully the procedure itself was a complete success and I recovered, but even so, I felt something was still not quite right. Two years later I had another operation to remove an excessive amount of suture that had been left in me!

The amount they removed would have rewound a cotton reel. Maybe they had no scissors in the operating theatre and just stuffed it inside my stomach!

The following morning, when I awoke, I was feeling very sorry for myself, but the morphine was helping, apparently I looked horrendous, my right eye was in the middle of a very large black and blue head, hair full of glass with cuts and bruises. I had pipes going in and out of every orifice, some of which were manmade!!

The first person to visit me was Sandy – I remember asking him how he was allowed in, to which he replied "I said I was your brother." Understand, he didn't look a bit like me, so I said "Sandy you don't look a bit like me". He bent down and whispered into my ear, "I f****** hope not!" I started to laugh and realised what a painful mistake it was, despite the morphine! Everyone, I feel, is lucky to have a friend such as he.

By Christmas, I had lost two stone, as I was eating and drinking very little in order to get used to my new, smaller intestinal system, but, other than that, I was fine and went back to work in the hotel, which Sandy and Sarah had been running very competently.

Whilst my relationship with Mandy was blossoming, she, quite naturally, was still worried about our age gap, so she asked my mum, now aged 82, what she thought about it. Mum sagely replied, "Well dear, it's better to be an old man's darling than a young man's slave." I think mum clinched it for me, for which I am eternally grateful.

Since dad had died, mum had found it a little hard to adjust as most of her life had been about looking after dad. He made all the decisions and mum would scurry around doing all the preparations. Memories of trips to the beach as children would be of dad carrying his chair and rolled Telegraph and pen whilst mum would look like a pack horse with everything a family of four would need for the beach.

For ten years or so they owned a villa in Menorca and I remember dad saying once "Joan, I'm fed up of making decisions, you decide where we go today". "OK Arthur", says mum, "Let's go to Son Bou" "Son Bou, Son Bou" says dad, "That's the single worst beach on the island." "Well, you asked me to make a decision" says mum, dad replies "Well, not if you're going to make silly ones like that!" and I don't think mum was allowed to make another decision for some time!

They sold the villa and then spent January and February in the Caribbean. I would meet them at Heathrow, and wait at the end of a long line of people who were waiting to greet their friends or family.

Then dad appeared, marching around the corner, he would wave his newspaper when he caught my eye at the end of the line. Ten yards behind would be mum, battling with an overladen trolley. But mum wouldn't have wanted it any other way. Dad was her reason for life.

After dad died, mum moved back to Knutsford to be near Letty who looked after her very well. Mum and dad had been living in their bungalow in St. David's for the past 25 years. Mum now embarked on her trips – she would stay with friends or go on holidays with them.

She went to Houston, in Texas to see one of her dearest friends, Joy Fontes, and having just left Houston, a young lady asked if she would mind swapping seats as mum was sitting next to her boyfriend. Mum, preferring an aisle seat was hesitant to move. "Where is your seat", she enquired? "In first class", came the reply.

Well, mum was out of her seat and into first class quicker than a cork out of a bottle! I asked mum what it was like. "Well, dear", she said "after the Champagne, caviar and chablis, I really can't remember."

There are two stories I love about mum. Firstly, one day she reversed into her neighbour's car causing about £500 worth of damage. We decided it might be better to pay up in case her insurance company wanted her to take another test. Three days later she rang me in an excitable state and said, 'Darling, the most marvellous thing has happened, someone has driven in to my neighbour's car (no one in it, I hasten to add) and written it off – I don't have to pay a thing!!!'

The second goes as follows: Whilst aged about 81, she drives her neighbour, Mrs Simpson (about 90) to Haverfordwest train station to see her best friend, Joy Fontes (about 85) off to London. Mum goes on the train to settle her in her seat and off sets the train! Mum quickly pulls the cord, the train stops, and then politely asks the conductor to reverse back to the station. This he could not do, but he would stop the train four miles up the track at the next station, Clarbeston Road, for mum to alight. Mum gets off the train and proceeds to the post office to ask for a taxi, giving her name. 'Are you Andrew's mother?' she is asked, 'Yes.' she says. 'Don't worry, I'll run you back to Haverfordwest.'. When back at her car, Mrs Simpson asks her why she was so long…!

In July 2002, Mum and Joy went to Lake Marjorie in northern Italy. "We had a marvellous holiday" she told Letty, when being wheeled off the plane at Manchester with both her elbows and knees in bandages from various falls. Mum had been suffering with cancer, but had always vowed never to be a burden to her family, so hadn't allowed the doctor to tell us. She always said, "I just wake up in the morning, give myself a good shake, and get on with the day." Definitely one of a kind.

She then decided to write to all the people she knew and embarked on a trip, in her car, around Britain to meet family and friends. On arriving in Bristol to stay with her sister, Aunty D, I had a phone call from cousin Anna to say that mum really wasn't that well and they had taken her to hospital. I went to see mum, I must admit, she looked tired, but I never thought she would be dead within the week. She was taken back to Cheshire where she sadly passed away, the end of a great lady.

Just before she went to Lake Marjorie, I remember Letty asking me how much money mum had left, I told her that this was the last holiday she could afford – from now on we will have to pay for her trips – so mum planned it perfectly and made the sorting out of the Will a very easy affair.

Mum's funeral was an emotional, but jolly occasion, even better because mum had asked our cousin Elizabeth (Libby) to sing in the church. Libby is an accomplished opera singer and, bless her, is asked to sing at various family occasions. But, of course, for no money.

In memory of mum, I decided to hold an annual light opera evening which Libby – paid this time – would bring her soprano friend, Anzy, and sing some beautiful, popular operatic arias. We held these evenings for several years, they were a great success, added to this it allowed me to catch up with Libbie, a truly lovely and generous-of-spirit individual.

Down Under

In 2003 Mandy announced that she was going to Australia for six months. She had spent 12 terms in Bartholomew School in Oxford and had decided to take some time out before settling down. I loved Oxford, Mandy had rented a shared flat in Whitney to start with and then she rented, on her own, a flat in Summertown, North Oxford.

I would spend half of my week in Wolfscastle and then drive to Oxford and spend the rest of

Walking up Ayres Rock

Elephant riding in Thailand

Sailing in the Whitsunday Islands

the week there. We would eat out, go punting, well, if anyone can do that successfully I take my hat off to them, and I actually spent quite a bit of my time playing squash, against other teachers from Bartholomew, going to the gym and walking – happy days.

As Mandy prepared for Australia, I asked if I could come too – she thought I would never leave my business for six months, but I knew that if she went, we would probably never get together.

So I suggested we condensed the six-months to three, Mandy created the itinerary, we stayed in youth hostels, which whilst being basic were, very clean, most of the time we had our own room and sometimes en-suite.

We ate out every night as, at that time, Australia and New Zealand were half the price of Britain. For £35 you could have an excellent quality meal for two and bottle of quality local wine.

We spent two days in Singapore and then for five weeks spent time in Australia. We started in Perth then flew to Alice Springs. I never forget the menu in a restaurant in Alice Springs – the first seven meat dishes, alligator, emu, kangaroo etc. I had never seen them on a menu before. I think I had the vegetarian dish, to play it safe.

We then travelled by bus from Alice Springs to Ayers Rock – it took a few hours and we were well entertained by the large Aussie bus driver who had formerly been a very capable Aussie rules football player. From what I could gather, it was a game of rugby combined with football and no rules – anyway – he regaled us with stories of his trip around Australia – which took him three years in a motorhome.

That's the thing about Australia, you look at the map and decide to do a small detour, only to find it takes half a day – we nearly ran out of petrol on one of these detours when travelling to Brisbane from Cairns. Well, back to the bus, from Alice Springs to Ayers Rock there is only one corner, and of course our driver thought it was hilarious to warn all his passengers that a corner was coming up.

He also acted as the postman, so every now and then he stopped and put post into someone's post-box at the end of the drive of a huge farm. On one occasion I noticed he came to an abrupt stop, made a sharp retreat and threw the post at the box. On returning I asked him why he had done that and he said, "A large brownie (snake) was curled up right under the post-box and you don't mess with them little f.......!"

After Ayres Rock we flew to Cairns up to Cape Tribulation, back to Cairns and then down to Brisbane and finally Sydney – stopping at most places in between – Mandy did all the bookings and created the agenda, I just shut up and drove! In fact, the only time we fell out was when I told her I was fed up of being told what to do all the time.

Maybe I had been divorced too long! She handed me the Lonely Planet Guide. "OK" she said "You make the decisions." I quietly apologised and handed her back the book! In fact, we didn't have another disagreement, I was so enjoying myself, relaxed, in a fantastic environment and with the woman of my dreams; what more could a man ask for.

Las Vegas with Lisa and Dean

Starting our four-day hike – South Island NZ

The Grand Canyon

Climbing the Sydney Harbour Bridge

We spent one of our last few days in Sydney with friends that Mandy had made in Oxford and were so sad to be leaving for Auckland in NZ. We had climbed Ayres Rock, the Sydney Harbour Bridge, cruised around the Whitsunday Islands and stopped off at Byron Bay, Frazer Island and many other great places, sheer heaven.

We arrived in NZ and stayed for a couple of days with a friend who had worked for me in the 80s at Wolfscastle, called Sara. She had married a local policeman and was living just south of Auckland. At first, because we had so enjoyed Australia, we felt that maybe NZ was going to be a bit of a let-down, but by the time the five weeks was up, we couldn't decide which country was the best. We hired an old Mazda and drove around all of the north and south islands, we covered over 2,000 miles and saw all the main attractions and went on some amazing walks.

For four days with Sara, her sister in law and mother in law, Gareth who had taught with Mandy in Oxford and had taken two years out to live and work in NZ, and his wife, Ceri who is sadly no longer with us, we walked part of the Routeburn track in South Island.

We took mud baths in Rotorua, what a smell! – walked the Tongariro Crossing (five hours up, three hours down) and before going to South Island we stopped off at Napier. After Mandy had awoken me at 6 o'clock in the morning so she could go and swim with dolphins – of no interest to me – we went on to Craggy Range to look around the vineyard – of interest to me – where Mike Llewellyn – my very good friend and occasional golfing partner, as well as being our wine merchant, had arranged for us to be "entertained".

We had a couple of their wines on our list at the hotel, but nothing compared to some of the wines our attentive host gave us to try. I remember trying a Pinot Noir that compared very favourably to when, as a student, I went with my mother, to be "lunched" by some of dad's wine merchant friends in Liverpool and drank Pommard, Clos Vougeot, Romani Conti and the like.

At Craggy Range we had probably one of the finest meals I have ever eaten, and at a vineyard – how perfect! We then crossed over to South Island and took a catamaran down the Abel Tasman – bungee jumped in Queenstown (Mandy, not me!!- she also did a skydive off Mission Beach in Australia!) and climbed the Franz Joseph glacier, amongst many other amazing things. In fact, thanks to Mandy's planning, every day was different and exciting.

It was with a heavy heart that we boarded the plane to finish the last leg of our trip – eight days in Thailand. We stayed one night in Bangkok, a smog-ridden place, we went round the Grand Palace, which was interesting, but immediately, when you left, locals tried to sell you their tacky wares. I was glad to get out and fly to Ko Samui – a small island to the south. The only two things I remember of our time here was, one, going on an elephant ride, which I didn't like, Mandy loved it, of course, but I kept wanting to jump off. I used to have that urge on ski lifts, neither a good idea.

The second memory was the trip to Ko Panyang. This was a two-hour boat trip in a relatively large, very old, open decked ferry with a canopy over, which did have an enclosed area as well. It wallowed its way across quite a bumpy sea to its smaller sister island. Halfway across, we were hit by a squall, I stupidly thought the canopy would be sufficient to keep me dry, instead, I might just as well have stood in a power shower. I pretended I loved getting absolutely soaked by the tropical rain.

We arrived at this small island and, with our backpacks, walked the mile to the other side of the island where we booked into a little house on stilts, on the beach, for the grand sum of £10, the best accommodation available. We then proceeded to the beach bar – a rundown shack at the top of the beach, but it did have a television, small and old, as at 6 o'clock they were showing the final of the World Rugby final, England v Australia.

We met up with a couple of backpackers, a Mancunian Pakistani and a Spanish guitarist, real characters whom we had a great afternoon with. The heavens opened and the television struggled to keep its picture, but it was good enough for us to see Jonny Wilkinson kick the winning points.

As in all tropical places the torrential rain abated as quickly as it had appeared and suddenly coloured mats and lanterns appeared on the beach – it was now dark – and a fire juggler was doing an impressive display and the four of us sat on our mat and drank buckets of alcohol, literally – you ordered a bucket of drink which contained rice whiskey, some sort of speed drink and four straws and we settled down to enjoy a full moon party.

By 3 o'clock, I decided to try and get Mandy back along the beach to our hut, she had started talking to the waves, the moon and giggling uncontrollably. I literally had to drag her, but eventually we made the hut. The next day we had to walk the mile back to the boat. It was as much as Mandy could do to carry herself, so I carried her backpack as well as my own and a few hours later we arrived, exhausted, back at Ko Samui.

Our three-month break had come to an end and it had cost very little considering everything we had done. I had realized how easy it was to live with Mandy and had even suggested on the top of Ayers Rock that maybe she would like our relationship to be a lifelong event, she told me she would consider it, but I would have to wait!

Back to Wales

Whilst we were away, son Ben, who was at Clifton College and aged 13 had been caught smoking on the roof of the school and had fallen through it and landed in the housemaster's daughter's bedroom which nearly resulted in him being expelled!!

He eventually achieved well at Clifton and went to Sheffield University where he succeeded in getting a 2:1, the only Stirling to get a degree! Tom had gone to Worcester University, having received a sports scholarship and was playing for Worcester Town under 21s.

He had been captain of rugby at Christ College in Brecon and was quite a formidable player – I had jokingly said, when he first went to Worcester, on being asked what course he was doing, "probably Women and Drinking".

The induction lady and I chuckled, Tom looked a little embarrassed, but that is exactly what he did – so whilst his rugby career started well, like with so many talented youngsters, life got in the way. Like father, like son, possibly!

Mandy decided she wanted to live in Cardiff, so we rented a flat and she started applying for jobs whilst registered on the supply list. Cardiff was halfway to Oxford, so much nearer to Wolfscastle – I was happy.

Eventually she secured a full-time job at Westbourne School in Penarth near Cardiff and rather than pay rent every month, we transferred it to a mortgage and bought a small house in the Canton area of the city.

The next four years were very enjoyable and like with Oxford, I could write a whole book on our life there. We met up with a group of people, some of whom we had known before, school friends of Mandy's as well, all of them either coming from or having connections with Pembrokeshire.

One couple that we spent a lot of time with were Charlie and Anna. Charlie was the son of two friends of mine, Dickie and Jill Parry who lived in Little Milford, just outside Haverfordwest. Dickie sadly died in 2016 of Motor Neurone disease, a very cruel disease.

We have been on many trips together and to date, we have been on two holidays, to Ischgl, skiing and Majorca. The weekend trips have been to London, Bruges, Rome, Bath and Dublin, all hilarious, we so enjoy their company, but I will allude to one – Bath.

The girls wanted to go to Bath Spa and have a spa day so Charlie and I decided to go racing. This meant finding a pub close to a bookies. We found the ideal venue and opposite was a bookies, so at 12 o'clock with all the racing papers to hand, we started studying the form.

Five hours later, everyone in the pub was giving us advice, we had consumed a considerable amount of alcohol and were only a few pounds out of pocket – the last race saved us! Enter the girls, refreshed, sober, and ready for a good night. I was relatively coherent, I had slowed down on the drink and even had a couple of pints of water – not so Charlie.

A decent proposal

We went to a restaurant and Charlie had randomly invited a young Australian couple to join us, then decided to disappear to buy a packet of cigarettes. My phone rang and a voice slurred, "Where are you?" "In the restaurant, of course," I giggled! "Yes, I know, but what is it called and where is it?" – Charlie was lost. Anyway, a great day eventually came to an end, but Charlie was told to sleep on the floor!

Another two dear friends, Sian and Chris also lived in Canton, easy walking distance for us, so several great evenings were had in each other's houses. On Mandy's 30th birthday, she told me that if I asked her again to marry me, she might say yes. A year earlier, we had a two-week holiday taking in Dubai, Mauritius, and the Seychelles, when I had again been told I would have to wait. So I was delighted that the time was now right.

A ring was bought and it was decided that a weekend in Paris would be the place to present it. Chris and Sian came with us and I booked a table in Paris' oldest restaurant called 'La Bofinger'.

It had to be in a catering establishment, where I was going to officially ask Mandy to marry me. Well, what a mess, the dessert arrived, I took out the ring, burst into tears, mumbled to Mandy would she marry me, Mandy burst into tears, mumbling yes, Sian burst into tears, realising the enormity of the occasion, whilst Chris, who had been distracted at the time had missed what was going on and looked on in amazement at three crying people. The tables adjacent to us were wondering what Chris had said to make three people burst into tears!

A date was set, 31st March 2007, some 14 months hence. Now marriage was really going to happen, we decided that all my savings should be put into buying a ski apartment in France; we chose France because I could speak some French and we loved the food.

Both Mandy and I had had a few skiing holidays, so what better than having a bolthole in the three valleys, the largest ski area in the Alps and a place we had holidayed a few times. We, actually, never saw the apartment until it was nearly built and virtually paid for, but it was a good choice. Unfortunately, we have had to recently sell it as the money was needed for hotel improvements.

The first time I skied was in 1959, just before my parents went into the catering trade, it was in Zurs, Austria and resulted in my ending up in plaster for two weeks as I tore the ligaments in my knee. But, over the years, I have had many skiing holidays and many laughs. A few antics that come to mind are Roger Balls doing a complete sideways 360, landing on his skis and standing like he'd meant to do it and David Crawford, a vet from Ayre, taking a child off a button lift whilst out of control. Susie McNair, who sadly broke her leg and is convinced that it only happened as it was the only time in her life she skied sober and, finally, Sandy coming off a slope and completely immersing himself in a snowdrift and getting annoyed with me as I was laughing so much I was incapable of helping him out.

The wedding was drawing nigh and, of course, poor old Libby was asked to sing in the church. My sister and I, in 1963, went to the cinema in Liverpool to watch "The Sound of Music" where we both proceeded to cry our eyes out, so "Climb Every Mountain" was chosen as one of the songs. I managed to just avert tears as Libby turned, lovingly, towards Mandy and I in mid-voice, but it was all too much for Letty, who failed to hold back tears for most of the song. It definitely was the best day of my life, it's a shame you can't repeat it every year.

We decided, before we settled down to married life to have a rather expensive two-week honeymoon, so first stop, three days in Victoria Falls. The locals were so nice and welcoming. I could fully understand why Uncle Leader spent his whole life with people such as these, then three days at Ulusaba, Richard Branson's Game Resort.

He was there at the time, very charming, if we had stayed one more evening we would have been invited to his relations' birthday party. Again, the people were amazing. The minute we arrived you were asked what drinks you wanted when you returned from a drive. During the

The 'Parry's' Dickie and Jill (below) Charlie and Anna (above and below)

Above – with Sian and Chris. Mandy and I got engaged two minutes before this picture was taken.

Outside Buckingham palace before going in to have tea with the Queen (with a couple of thousand other people!)'

My beautiful wife

Master of ceremonies, best man and ushers

Possibly the best day of my life

Jenny & David Harries – the 'in-laws'.
Some hat Jenny!

drive, a refreshment was on hand for when we stopped for a break.

I chose a South African red, Mandy a sauvignon blanc – and from then on copious amounts of each were on tap, well, I needed it, being driven around in a zoo full of dangerous animals in an open top jeep and no fences was not my idea of fun. I couldn't get back to camp for my dinner quick enough where stories that enhanced my doubts of the safety of such holidays were regaled. Only two weeks earlier a pride of lions had taken up camp by the swimming pool, so it was out of use – I didn't go near it – and a leopard had wandered through the open air dining area whilst everyone was having dinner! You were escorted back to your "hut" by a guy with a gun – and you made sure everything was locked or else the baboons might ravage your room, which happened to a couple a few weeks prior.

The baboons did have a party on our roof one morning, which frightened the life out of me. The funniest thing, during our three nights at Ulusaba was when, one evening, talking with the young New Zealand lady chef whilst reading the menu, I noticed she had put down as one of the starters – snails. "Odd choice", I said as I studied the nine other guests. "They are delicious", she replies "I am sure they are, but against the other starters, no one will have them."

So I suggested that if no one ordered them, offer them as an amuse bouche to everyone, including our two hosts, Patience and James. No one did order any, so out came 13 snails. Most people ate one, but James was hilarious, we tried and tried to get him to eat his, he would put it in his mouth, but that is as far as it went – a great fun evening.

We then flew down to Capetown to stay with an old friend of mine, Andy Whipp. I had known Andy since 1960 and during my school years. We played golf together in the holiday times. We spent a great few days, doing the usual sightseeing, and took in a couple of vineyards – one whose wines I had on my wine list, so we were given a private tour and then lunch was provided where lobster, I remember was given to us, most enjoyable.

Before we flew back to Britain, we relaxed for a few days in Mauritius, in one of the sumptuous hotels on the island. I am not over-comfortable staying in a place where real poverty abounds, does the money you spend stay on the island, does it give meaningful employment? I don't know. I will say that Richard Branson helped the village adjacent to his game resort and everyone looked very happy and cared for. So, maybe, some people are doing things for the betterment of the local community, I hope so.

The generation game

In February 2008, Mandy announced she was pregnant. We hadn't really discussed children, I am not sure we would have bought the ski apartment, if we had, as my idea was to escape to it for the month of January, and really improve my skiing; not possible with a baby on board.

On September 11th, out popped Oliver William Stirling. I remember Mandy in the birthing pool in Withybush Hospital, exhausted but elated, hugging me and Ollie and all of us howling our eyes out. What a special moment. What women have to do to give birth. If it was down to men, I think the human race would have come to an abrupt halt!

We had decided that living in Cardiff was no longer an option, Ollie had nearly been born in Cardiff as I remember we had gone to a Thai restaurant and my eldest, Tom, had joined us, where some spicy food was devoured. Mandy then had a rather uncomfortable night which we blamed on the meal.

But, not convinced this was caused by the food, maybe the baby was coming early, we decided to head west. I, however, had to go to Macro to buy some things for the hotel, Mandy decided to stay in the car as she was getting more uncomfortable. When I returned, she announced that she was having regular contractions I drove quite quickly to Pembrokeshire and Ollie joined the world the following morning at 10am.

Brothers in arms

In 2009, my great friend Sandy died. We had been best friends since 1967 and, in fact, for the first ten years of our friendship, we had seen each other every day and his last twelve years,

James in Ulasaba never ate the snail!

very nearly the same. Even the twenty years in between, we met frequently, so when he had said "I said I was your brother" to the nurse when visiting me in hospital after my accident, he most surely was.

Sandy was a big smoker and in May, he was diagnosed with a brain tumour, which was successfully removed, however, he also had nodes on his lungs and kidneys so started a course of chemotherapy which seemed to be going well. In late October, on returning from a weekend away, I was told he had been admitted to hospital. In I went, to find a cheerful Sandy who thought that the slight bleeding he was experiencing was due to the chemo having done its job and the tumour was breaking up.

It took me until Wednesday to find a doctor who would tell me what was going on – again you had to be a relation, so Sandy told the doctor I was like a brother and could be told anything. The doctor took me into a side room and told me he was being sedated as he only had a week to live and a week later, he died.

It was the saddest day of my life, I howled. Sandy had three sisters, Ann, Mary and Alison. Mary had been knighted for services to the NSPCC. She was the chief executive and all three of them, like his parents, were lovely people. It was felt that as I knew Sandy, probably better than anyone, that I would give the eulogy.

I don't think I slept for the five days before the funeral as I wrote and rewrote the words and paced up and down reading them, never quite being able to get to the last paragraph. On the day, all went well, the eulogy was all about the amusing things we had done, but I didn't manage to finish the last paragraph – anyway – I had a standing ovation, whether it was out of sympathy or because I executed it well, I'll never know!

Looking back I was glad that in the year before his death, we had spent a week together skiing, at the apartment.

Sandy hadn't skied for some time so was a little rusty and on the second lift of the day he didn't move across enough to allow me to get on, so I gave him a slight nudge, he fell over, along came the chair, which I duly sat on, with Sandy squashed underneath it. The lift was stopped and Sandy was ignominiously extracted. He thought I had done it on purpose so for a few minutes the atmosphere was a little tense, but by the first pit stop we were laughing about it.

On the first holiday after Sandy's death Mandy and I, on reaching the top of the first lift of the day, the one prior to Sandy's escapade, I tried to get off the lift, and couldn't, I had to throw myself to the ground, otherwise I would have gone back down. Mandy and I looked at each other and both said "Sandy". That has never happened before or since and I have been on hundreds and hundreds of chair lifts, so what other explanation is there – he had a wicked sense of humour.

In 2009, on returning from a weekend with Charlie and Anna in Bruges, Mandy had a notion that she might be pregnant again, so went to the chemist and tested herself. She was – more tears and hugging and seven months later on January 16th 2010, out popped Robbie.

Time for an upgrade

The turnover at Wolfscastle was depleting year on year as little investment had been made, so we decided that as now we had two small boys, we needed to upgrade both our house and the hotel The house in Cardiff was sold and in 2013, we built the Brasserie followed in 2014 with extending and completely revamping the function suite.

We had previously spent time and money on the bedrooms, toilets, restaurant, kitchen, so by 2016, we felt we had a product that competed well in all areas; the downside is a large loan from HSBC! But thanks must go to Jane Rees, the bank manager, who has been very supportive.

We need now to upgrade some of the bedrooms still and in 2017, if cash allows, we are hoping to build some treatment rooms to offer to guests and locals alike.

Mandy, has orchestrated all the changes with help from Linda Hunt, our interior designer. Mandy has banned me, quite rightly, from making any improvement suggestions and her good taste has prevailed.

Everything is now painted with contemporary colours so not to impose on bride's colour schemes – gone are my red chairs and red and white striped canopy, for instance, as has just about everything else I installed before meeting her, including the clowns! I have to say she is right, but when is a woman not?!

There is little more to say, other than it is now nearly Christmas 2017, and where has it all gone, life is so short and my only advice I would give to my children is don't waste time, don't leave off for tomorrow what you can do today. Be decent, honest, true people and achieve whatever it is you aspire to. I remember my dad telling me I couldn't shoot a gun (I used to like shooting, targets mainly, birds were pretty safe) until I could recite "If" by Rudyard Kipling – so some years ago I gave it to my two older boys to read – here it is:

If you can keep your head when all about
Are losing theirs and blaming it on you,
If you can trust yourself when all men doubt you,
But make allowances for their doubting too;
If you can wait and not be tired by waiting,
Or being lied about, don't deal in lies,
Or being hated, don't give way to hating,
And yet don't look too good, nor talk too wise:

If you can dream – and not make dreams you master;
If you can think – and not make thoughts your aim;
If you can meet Triumph and Disaster
And treat those two imposters just the same;
If you can bear to hear the truth you've spoken
Twisted by knaves to make a trap for fools,
Or watch the things you gave your life to, broken,
And stoop and build 'em up with worn-out tools:
If you can make one heap of all your winnings
And risk it on one turn of pitch-and-toss,
And lose, and start again at your beginnings
And never breathe a word about your loss;
If you can force your heart and nerve and sinew
To serve your turn along after they are gone,
And so hold on when there is nothing in you
Except the will which says to them: 'Hold on!'

If you can talk with crowds and keep your virtue,
Or walk with Kings – nor lose the common touch,
If neither foes nor loving friends can hurt you
If all men count with you, but not too much;
If you can fill the unforgiving minute
With sixty seconds' worth of distance run,
Yours is the earth and everything that's in it,
And – which is more- you'll be my man, my son!

Our latest addition, Freddie the golden cocker on
Newgale beach

With Thanks

To conclude, there are so many people I have omitted, but this book is just a snapshot of
a life and a list of dishes that have inspired me, but there are a few people I feel I need to
mention.

The Sykes family, Martin, Cecelia, Rupert, Lotty, Ed and Louise and Gay – Martin Sykes needs
to write a book, I'd love to read that. I have skied a few times with him and sailed around
the Med. His company is electric and definitely someone who hasn't stood still. Ed and Lou,
great weekend in London and Lotty, now married to Andrew, lovely lady. Mike Llewellyn,
married to lovely Judy, my wine merchant for years, always a huge supporter of the hotel and
someone whom I have played much golf with, thank you Mike and Judy for your friendship.

Brian and Margaret Harries, many charities owe a lot to these two as they run so
many auctions at the hotel and together increase the amount raised through Brian's
persuasiveness, whilst Margaret ensures that the right monies are extracted – so much
thanks to you guys. Brian Mutton, sadly deceased, Mike Williams, Rob Moffat, Tony Reyland,
Roger Burns and Richard Mee – all squash team members I played with in the 1980s; my life

has been enriched by knowing you – many thanks and thanks to their long-suffering wives as well. I remember having a friendly argument with a team member, Alwyn Vaughan, best friend of Brian Mutton, at the bar one day about a matter to do with squash, looking to his friend for support, Brian says in his Swansea accent, "Well, you see, it's like this, Alwyn, when I was a boy, as you know, I lived in a street in Swansea, and there was one boy who owned a football, so, whenever we wanted to play we had to befriend him and invite him to play." "What's this got to do with it?" says Alwyn, "Well, Alwyn", says Brian, looking at me, "It's his football." What a lovely guy he was.

Also, at about this time, a young RAF pilot called Davi d Keenan, with his wife Chrissie, would spend many happy hours at the hotel, playing squash. Chrissie sadly died, so we invited Chris Mutton, (Brian's wife) and Dave Keenan to a dinner party to celebrate Brian and Chrissie's lives. It was a lovely, but very emotional evening. I hadn't seen Dave for over 20 years. He then decided to move back and live in Wolfscastle. A friend who had helped him walking his five dogs after Chrissie had died, came to visit him, a lovely lady called Sue, and she didn't go back. They lived in Wolfscastle for five years, Dave having retired as a Wing Commander. They have now moved to live in Stroud.

Thanks to Cousin Sally who helped me get started at Wolfscastle and Cousin Jackie and Peter, who offered help when I was a bit stuck recently – true, true friends!

Finally, I would like to thank my "in-laws" and brother-in-law, Paul, for being so supportive. Without their support, I would never have been allowed to marry Mandy. David, or Dai, as he is known, is of farming stock, who still works even though he is in his mid-seventies. Like myself, he will probably still be doing his job when his time is up, simply because it is our "raison d'etre". Jenny, his lovely lady wife whom Dai said at our wedding is "his rock". And, Paul, Mandy's elder brother. As with so many Welsh families, they are well knitted and without their approval, your chances of being accepted are very slim.

Thank you to all the people that have made my life so fulfilling, and most of all, my adorable wife Mandy, I love you so much and my four gorgeous boys – you have given me SO many memorable moments.

Finally, thank YOU for buying this book, I hope it has given you some entertainment and some useful recipes.

So, That's What it's All About!

Ollie and Robbie in the alps

Mandy, Ollie, Robbie and I on Mandy's 40th birthday

One last thing

By way of summary and a final window into my views on life, I thought I would indulge myself in answering a few questions that you sometimes ask yourself.

Q: "Who has had the most influence on you in your life?"

AS: The answer, for me, would be four people; my parents, my soul brother Sandy and my wife Mandy.

I grew up watching my parents develop a business – my father was totally fair and very direct – an intelligent man who did not suffer fools gladly. Not everyone liked him, as I think his father had put a few gremlins into his head which made him quite awkward at times. But when it came to honesty, truthfulness and fair mindedness, he was all those things. I so admired him.

My mother, was a more rounded character, she could laugh at herself, something dad struggled with – and she had a real work ethic. Her job, she felt, was to do whatever dad required of her and look after him and whilst he could be quite, unwittingly, mentally cruel to her at times, she never failed from her duty.

Duty is definitely the word that defined her. Everyone loved mum, she had quite Victorian principles, but she managed to adapt them to modern life and I know Letty, myself and her grandchildren adored her.

Sandy, well, you don't often get as good a friend as he was to me, just a thoroughly decent guy, I suppose. Whilst I see myself as being reasonably intelligent, I am not intellectual, whereas Sandy thrived on absorbing literature, he wasted much of his intellect on trivia, but it made such an interesting and fun guy to be around.

I remember once mixing up my metaphors and suggesting to Sandy that we shouldn't "shoot the golden goose in the foot," "interesting" says Sandy, would that be "shooting the golden goose that lays the golden eggs" or "shooting ourselves in the foot". Such a witty guy, I was so lucky to have known him.

And then my wife Mandy, she came into my life in the late 1990s and we became an "item" in the year 2000. I was always lacking confidence but she has given it back to me, I don't know where I would be without her.

Q: Who would you like to come to dinner?

AS: I hear people, quite often pondering this question, and most of us would say Nelson Mandela, he appears to be the modern Jesus – a man persecuted yet able to forgive. It's so sad, I feel, that we don't appear to learn from such people. We all admire their great attributes, but too few of us adhere to them.

Anyway, on a lighter note – Gordon Ramsey would be another one. Every time I watch his

"Kitchen Nightmares" television programme, I so agree with what he says about the catering trade and I love his passion for food.

The same could be said for Keith Floyd – I would like to have spent more time with him – a real character. Of course, it would have to be a banquet and last for months!

Q: What are your favourite places?

AS: Having spent more than two-thirds of my life in West Wales, I think, maybe this is one of the nicest places on the planet. I don't queue well and living in a metropolis queuing is something you have to suffer on a daily basis.

Fresh air, walking Freddie our spaniel dog along Newgale beach on a spring day when the tide is out, leaving endless acres of sand and the sun peeking out from behind a few cirrus clouds. But best of all, there is hardly anyone else there, just you, your thoughts and a crazy dog! But, I have to admit, skiing in the Alps comes a close second, along with sitting on a hot sandy beach; Greek islands have always been my favourite destination – and walking through French or Spanish markets, taking in the smells and the atmosphere.

The more I think about it, the more I like a whole host of places. As I get older, I think "the like" bit comes from the fact I am in a very happy place in my life and as long as I have my wife and my children with me – I pretty much love anywhere!

Q: What are your most memorable moments?

AS: I have been lucky, I think our generation have seen so much change and diversity that the modern generation will not experience – sadly.

Playing rugby in my teens was a great experience. I remember the last match of the season against Downside; we had not been beaten and nor had they. Our No. 10 was a lad called Paul Kent, whose brother Charles went on to play for England, but Paul was equally as capable, so making our job that bit easier.

With 15 minutes to go we were one try down – I was playing No. 7 and as the ball came out of the scrum I managed to get a foot to it and from the halfway line, dribbled it to the try line – I was quite an adept sprinter – dived and was awarded the try! We didn't convert, but it meant it was a draw – 'Hero Stirling' had saved the day!

I have many, many, happy squash moments – beating the Welsh U17 champion to get to the last sixteen of the Welsh closed being one, winning the Cardigan, Carmarthen & Pembrokeshire over-35 tournament three times and travelling with Cardiff Squash Club in Europe – great days – but, of course, my favourite dates have been the birth of my four sons and my marriage to Mandy on the 31st March 2007. If my life finished tomorrow I can't complain.

My wife with Stella's cake on her head!

Final thoughts

This bit is for my children – I hope I am seen as someone who has a half full and not half empty attitude, and doesn't take himself too seriously. I try to look at the whole world and show a bit of humility – we are so lucky compared to so many. When I hear someone complaining about something trivial, I want to say "go and complain to a small African child who walks 15 miles a day to fetch clean water and see what response you get".

Whilst not a practising Christian, I tend to only go to church for weddings, christenings and funerals – but, whether or not I believe in Christ, I believe a lot in what The Bible says with regards to The Ten Commandments and the Parables and the like. I think we all should read The New Testament – I was forced to at school – and whether you believe in God or not – trying to live one's life along the principles within the pages – is to be commended.

Well that's it. I think it always beneficial to learn from the people who have gone before, or at least from their mistakes! And I hope that ramblings about my life have been in some way helpful to you, and if not, that at least you will enjoy the recipes! Above all, if all else fails, try to have fun, as I have, and appreciate life, because as Plato said, 'Even the gods love jokes!"

Andrew Stirling

STARTERS
AND
SUNDRIES

Breakfast

When at St Non's and then in the early years at Wolfscastle I would be the breakfast chef. When cooking for a number the essence is to do your preparation, fry off your fried bread and colour your tomatoes and sausages in a frying pan. Then when the order comes in the bacon is grilled and the eggs are cooked in the desired fashion.

We use free range Burford brown eggs. They are expensive, but so worth the extra with their flavoursome deep yellow yolks. Personally, if cooking poached eggs I don't put vinegar in the water because it can taint the egg. Instead just drop the egg gently into a not-too-full pan of nearly boiling water gently and the egg should hold.

For scrambled eggs, add a little full fat milk and seasoning into your whisked eggs and pour into a pan when you have melted a knob of butter on a medium to low heat. Make sure that you stir enough so that the eggs are still runny but scrambled — you don't want pieces of omelette!

When an order comes in everything else — sausages, tomato, mushrooms and bacon — are grilled off and served.

Personally, I hate the buffets that large hotels have where everything is in chafing dishes, slowly drying up. For our black pudding, we buy a reasonably priced one and remake it, adding apple, onion and sweet spices. This gives it a more acceptable flavour to those who are not fans of black pudding and the likes of me that love it — it is still really tasty with a slight twist. I tell all our staff that breakfast is the last meal and memory of the hotel, so it has to be memorable. Even people who never eat a full breakfast at home find themselves ordering "the works" in a hotel. Indulge!

Canapes

We've amassed a selection of favourite canpes over the years. Though that selection is ever-evolving as we add more and more to it over time. Flavours from around the world, new ingredients and ideas from the kitchen help us to create delicious snacks for guests to enjoy at lunch, over dinner or during a special occasion.

The key to us is to keep our canapes light and playful – while making sure they are packed full of flavour. There ought to be great texture and the chance for people to enjoy a one-or-two-bite snack while enjoying themselves with family and friends.

Eggs benedict

Ingredients

Brioche bun halved
Ham, see Page 86

Poached eggs
1 ltr water
100ml white wine vinegar
or lemon juice
2 free range eggs

Hollandaise sauce
125g butter
2 egg yolk
½ tsp white wine vinegar
or tarragon vinegar
Pinch salt
Splash ice cold water
Lemon juice
Cayenne pepper

Method
(SERVES 2)

Poached eggs

1.   Bring the water and white wine vinegar/lemon juice to a rolling boil in a deep pan.

2.   Slowly break the eggs into the pan near the side and boil for 1 ½ minutes until the whites are firm.

3.   Remove from the water with a slotted spoon and place on a paper towel to drain. Serve immediately.

Hollandaise sauce

1.   Melt 125g of butter in a sauce pan and skim any white solids from the surface. Keep the butter warm. Put 2 egg yolks, ½ tsp white wine vinegar or tarragon vinegar, a pinch of salt and a splash of ice-cold water in a metal or glass bowl that will fit over a pan of barely simmering water and whisk continuously until pale and thick. It should take about 3-5 minutes.

2.   Remove from the heat and slowly whisk in the melted butter, bit by bit until it's all incorporated and you have a creamy hollandaise. If it gets too thick, add a splash of water. Season with a squeeze of lemon juice and a little cayenne pepper. Keep warm.

Brioche bun

1.   Toast the bun for 30 seconds. Be careful not to burn as brioche burns very quickly.

Assembly

1.   Place a slice of ham on one half of the bun, add the poached egg on top and coat with hollandaise.'

This is a lovely breakfast dish or lunchtime snack which has become more popular. The ham, of course is our own ham coupled with our homemade hollandaise and Burford brown free range eggs – with their deep yellow yolks. It makes an amazing dish.

Piccalilli and smoked chilli and red pepper chutney

Ingredients

Piccalilli, see Page 86

Smoked chilli and red pepper chutney
100g red chillies – halved and seeded
1.2kg vine tomatoes – quartered
600g red peppers – seeded and quartered
200g onion – finely diced
3tsp smoked paprika
50ml olive oil
1tsp caraway seed
6 cloves garlic – finely chopped
4 bay leaves
250g brown sugar
200ml red wine vinegar
Salt and pepper to taste

Method

1. Smoke the chillies and red pepper for 20-30 minutes, check to see if they have taken on a good, strong smoky flavour, or leave a little longer.

2. Roast the tomatoes in a hot oven until the edges colour a little.

3. In a large heavy based saucepan, fry the onion and garlic in the olive oil until translucent. Add the seeds and bay leaves and cook for a further 5 minutes taking care not to colour.

4. Pulse the chillies and peppers in a food processor leaving a bit of texture.

5. Add to the pan along with the tomatoes, brown sugar and vinegar, and simmer for an hour or so, stirring regularly, reducing to a pulpy chutney. Season with salt and pepper. Add paprika and cook for another 10 minutes.

6. Bottle in sterilized jars and keep for 2 weeks before opening.

Of course you can just buy these off us rather than go through the bother of making them – I like to think these are as good as you will get.

Smoked chili &
tomato chutney
gourmet to go
FROM THE KITCHEN AT
Wolfscastle
COUNTRY HOTEL
250g℮
Piccalilli
gourmet to go
FROM THE KITCHEN AT
Wolfscastle
COUNTRY HOTEL
250g℮

Honey glazed ham and piccalilli

Ingredients

Honey glazed ham

4kg Horseshoe Gammon
250g butter
200ml honey
Zest and juice of one orange
3 star anise
1tbsp coriander seed
1 inch cinnamon stick
8 cloves

Piccalilli

300g courgette, 1cm diced
300g cauliflower, 1cm florets
300g carrots, 1cm diced
300g shallots, thinly sliced
500g salt
2 small onions, diced
2 bay leaves
2g onion seeds
20g English mustard
180g sugar
50g honey
600g cider vinegar
30g cornflour
10g ground turmeric
10g ground ginger
5g ground cumin
5g ground coriander seed

Method
(SERVES 12)

Honey glazed ham

1. Boil the gammon for 4 hours in water. When done, remove from the water, de-skin and score.

2. Add all of the glaze ingredients together and bring to the boil in a large pan. Once all are combined into a liquid, pour over the ham. Roast on 140C for 40 minutes, and baste every 10 minutes until golden and sticky.

Piccalilli

1. Thoroughly salt the courgette, cauliflower, carrots and shallots in separate bowls and leave for 24 hours. After this is done, the salt can be washed from the vegetables with cold water. Drain the vegetables in a colander. In a large saucepan, fry the diced onion in a small amount of vegetable oil until the onions are soft and starting to brown.

2. Add the bay leaves, onion seeds, turmeric, cumin, coriander and ginger and continue to fry for 5 minutes stirring regularly.

3. Once the spices are well incorporated and the mixture is paste like, add the English mustard, sugar, honey and vinegar. Stir well and allow the mixture to simmer for 30 minutes.

4. In a bowl add a little water to the cornflour and stir into a paste. Add the paste to the sauce and stir well as it thickens. Continue to simmer and stir sauce for a further 10 minutes.

5. Add the salted vegetables to the sauce and take off the heat. The piccalilli is now ready for jarring in sterilized jam jars.

Honey glazed ham and piccalilli – a decent ham, not the watered stuff that you get in supermarkets, is a thing to enjoy. Add it to one of my favourite chutneys and you have a splendid lunch time snack.

French onion soup

Ingredients

50g butter
1 tbsp vegetable oil
1kg onion, halved and thinly sliced
1 tsp salt
4 garlic cloves, thinly sliced
2 tbsp plain flour
250ml dry white wine
1.3ltr hot, strongly flavoured beef stock
8 slices of French bread (depending on size)
140g Gruyere, finely grated
1/2 tbsp demerara sugar

Method
(SERVES 4)

1. Melt the butter with the oil in a large heavy-based pan. Add the onions and fry with the lid on for 10 minutes until soft. Sprinkle in the sugar and cook for a further 20 minutes, stirring frequently, until caramelized. The onions should be really golden, full of flavour and soft when pinched between your fingers. Take care towards the end to ensure they don't burn.

2. Add the garlic for the final few minutes of the onions' cooking time, then sprinkle in the flour and stir well. Increase the heat and keep stirring as you gradually add the wine, followed by the hot stock. Cover and simmer for 15-20 minutes.

3. To serve, turn on the grill, and toast the bread. Ladle the soup into heatproof bowls. Put a slice of toast on top of the bowls of soup, and pile on the cheese. Grill until melted. Alternatively, you can complete the toasts under the grill, then serve them on top.

I remember making this in St Non's in the early 1970s, but I didn't brown the onions enough so I liquidised it and served it as cream of onion soup. One guest said it was the nicest soup he had ever tasted, I didn't like to tell him it was a mistake.

Cold curried apple soup

Ingredients

50ml olive oil
1 diced onion
50g diced celery
½ minced garlic clove
1tsp curry powder
1ltr white chicken stock
400g cored and sliced
granny smith apples
600g cored and sliced gala
apples
Salt and pepper
½ juice of a lemon
100ml single cream

Method
(SERVES 4)

1. In a hot saucepan add the olive oil and cook the onion, celery and garlic until softened. Add the apples and cook gently until they break apart.

2. Add the curry powder and fry for 1 minute. Add the chicken stock and simmer for 20 minutes.

3. Blend the mixture in a food processor while still quite hot. Be careful when doing so, place a cloth on the lid and keep a firm grip to stop it exploding through the top.

4. Once the mixture is well blended, pass through a fine sieve and cool. Mix with the cream and season with salt, pepper and lemon to taste.

5. Garnish with finely diced cubes of apple mixed into the soup and dried apple slices.

One of my mum's favourite dishes, it is so good and yet it never sells when I put it on a modern menu!

Penderyn whisky cured salmon, blood orange, watercress puree, crème fraiche

Ingredients

Salmon

1kg side of salmon, pin boned and trimmed

200ml Penderyn single malt whisky

200g soft light brown sugar

200g Halen mon sea salt flakes

2 blood orange

Watercress puree

100g watercress

1% xanthan gum

Garnish

100ml crème fraiche

50g water cress

1 blood orange

Method
(SERVES 8)

Salmon cure

1. For the salmon cure, pin bone and trim the salmon fillet but leave the skin intact.

2. Mix the salt, sugar and whisky until well combined.

3. Zest, then slice the blood orange, and add the zest to the salt cure.

4. Using tin foil, wrap the salmon fillet tightly around the sides whilst leaving the flesh exposed and skin side down.

5. Carefully pat the cure mix on top of the salmon fillet, and lay the orange slices on top. Cover the cure with the cling film and weigh down with a smooth plate. Turn every 12 hours for at least 24 hours.

Watercress puree

1. Place the watercress in boiling water for 30 seconds, then put straight into an ice bath.

2. Scoop the watercress into a powerful blender with 1% of its weight in xanthan, blend, sieve, finished!

This is my present head chef Ian's dish – it tastes fabulous, and I love the colours.

Salmon gravlax

Ingredients

Red wine reduction
1 bottle red wine
280ml apple juice
100ml port
100ml red wine vinegar
500g brown sugar
5 star anise
5 tbsp coriander seeds
Pinch of salt

Pickled beetroot
500g fresh beetroot,
cleaned, top and tailed
100g Welsh butter

Beetroot puree
500g roast beetroot with
skin removed
100g butter
15ml balsamic vinegar
40ml water
Salt to taste

Horseradish cream
100ml double cream
1 tsp horseradish
1 tsp lemon juice
Season to taste

Lemon and saffron jelly
250ml granulated sugar
1 tsp grated lemon rind
175ml lemon juice
14g unflavoured gelatine
2 pinch saffron threads

Method
(SERVES 8)

Red wine pickle

1.   Place all ingredients in one pan and reduce on a medium heat until at a syrup consistency.

Pickled beetroot

1.   Place the beetroot for pickled and puree in a small tray. Melt the butter and pour over the beetroot, coating well. Cover the tray well with 2 layers of tin foil and roast in the oven on 140C for 2/2.5 hours until tender and the skin rubs off easily. Dice half the beetroot into 1cm cubes and place in pickle. Leave to pickle for 2 days before serving.

Beetroot puree

1.   With the remaining beetroot remove the skin and cut into half inch dice. Add all the ingredients together in a deep pan and cook for 10-15 minutes. Pour all into a food processor and blitz for 5 minutes until smooth and milky. Pass through a fine sieve and season to taste.

Horseradish cream

1.   Pass the horseradish through a fine sieve removing any horseradish chunks. Place all the ingredients together and whip to soft peaks. Cover and place in the fridge to firm up.

Lemon and saffron jelly

1.   Set aside 2 tbsp of the sugar. In a saucepan, combine the remaining sugar, rind and juice, and 750ml water and sprinkle the gelatine on top. Let stand for 5 minutes, then bring to simmer over a medium heat, stirring until the sugar and gelatine are dissolved.

2.   Remove from the heat, stir in the saffron, crumbing slightly with fingers. Pour into rinsed but not dried 1 or 1.25ltr mould or bowl. Let cool to room temperature. Cover and refrigerate until firm, at least 8 hours or overnight.

RECIPE CONTINUES OVERLEAF

Salmon gravlax

Salmon gravlax

75g sea salt

2 x 500g pieces skin-on organic salmon fillet, both cut from the centre of the fish. Ask your fishmonger to pin-bone it for you.

75g golden caster sugar

1 tsp black peppercorn, roughly crushed

Zest of 1 lemon

8 juniper berry, crushed (optional)

Small bunch (20g) dill, roughly chopped

2 tbsp gin

1. Pat the salmon dry with kitchen paper and run your hands over the flesh to see if there are any stray small bones – if there are, use a pair of tweezers to pull them out. Set the salmon fillets aside.

2. Tip the salt, sugar, peppercorns, lemon zest, juniper and dill into a food processor and blitz until you have a bright green, wet salt mixture or 'cure'. Unravel some cling film but keep it attached to the roll.

3. Lay the first fillet of salmon, skin side down and then pack the cure over the flesh. Drizzle with gin, if using, and top with the second fillet, flesh side down. Roll the sandwiched fillets tightly in cling film to create a package.

4. Place the fish in a shallow baking dish or shallow-sided tray and lay another tray on top. Weigh the tray down with a couple of tins or bottles and place in the fridge for at least 48 hours or up to 4 days, turning the fish every 12 hours or so. The longer you leave it the more cured it will become.

5. To serve, unwrap the fish and brush off the marinade with kitchen paper. Rinse if you like. You can slice the fish classically into long thin slices, leaving the skin behind or remove the skin and slice it straight down. Serve the sliced fish on a large platter or individual plates with pumpernickel bread, dill and mustard sauce.

Looks amazing and tastes amazing – if you want to impress at a dinner party all can be prepared a day or so ahead. Plate up, sit back and take the applause!

Coquilles St Jacques

Ingredients

8 scallops, live in the shell,
shell cleaned
200g button mushrooms,
thinly slices
¼ lemon, juice only
500ml fish stock

Potatoes
300g medium baking
potatoes
2 free range egg yolks
25g butter
Salt and freshly ground
white pepper

Sauce
50g butter
25g plain flour
2 free range egg yolks
150ml double cream
Salt and freshly ground
black pepper

Assembly
15g gruyere, finely grated
15g fine breadcrumbs
50g butter, melted
Salt and freshly ground
black pepper

Method
(SERVES 4)

1. Place the whole live scallops onto a hotplate or hot griddle pan for 1-2 minutes, until they begin to open.

2. Slide the blade of a filleting knife between the flat shell and the scallop and carefully lift off the shell lid.

3. Slide the knife blade between the scallop and the concave shell to detach the scallop and coral.

4. Keep the four best concave shell halves for serving. Brush them under cold water and dry them out.

5. Peel off the membrane surrounding the scallops, clean in cold water, cut in pieces and set aside for use in the sauce.

6. Separate the whites of the scallops from the orange corals and wash gently in cold water to remove any grains of sand.

7. Place the scallops, corals, mushrooms, membranes and lemon juice in a pan with the fish stock. Set over a low heat and slowly bring to the boil. Lower the heat to simmer very gently for one minute. Remove from the heat, set aside and keep the scallops and mushrooms in the stock at room temperature.

8. Preheat oven to 220C.

9. Scrub the potatoes under cold water and prick in 2-3 places with the point of a knife. Place onto a baking sheet and transfer to the oven to bake in their jackets for 35-40 minutes, or until soft inside.

10. Halve the potatoes and scoop out the cooked flesh from the jacket. Force the potato flesh through a hard sieve or ricer into a clean bowl.

11. Add two of the egg yolks and the butter and beat until smooth. Season to taste with salt and freshly ground white pepper. The potato can be done the day before and kept in the fridge until needed.

Sauce

1. Melt the butter in a saucepan, stir in the flour and cook for two minutes to make a roux.

2. Take the pan off the heat and strain in the stock from the scallops and mushrooms, stirring constantly to combine without lumps. Set the scallops and mushroom aside.

3. Simmer the sauce gently for a few minutes, whisking frequently.

4. In a bowl, mix the two egg yolks with the cream, then pour the mixture into the sauce. Before it begins to bubble, take the pan off the heat, season the sauce with salt and freshly ground black pepper and keep hot.

Assembly

1. Increase the oven temperature to 240C.

2. Cut the scallop whites into thick slices. Place a layer of mushrooms into each of the four clean scallop shells. Add 2 scallop whites then top with the scallop corals.

3. Fill a piping bag with the potato mixture and pipe an attractive ribbon around the edges of the scallop shells.

4. Mix the gruyere and breadcrumbs together in a clean bowl.

5. Cover the mushroom and scallop layers generously with sauce and sprinkle the top with the gruyere and breadcrumbs mixture.

6. Melt the butter and pour it over the top of the sauce.

7. Place the scallops into the hot oven to bake for 3-5 minutes, until the top of the sauce is lightly glazed and the potato border pale golden.

8. Do not forget to warn your guests that the scallop shell will be extremely hot.

I habitually ate this dish at the Leigh Arms, in Prestbury, in the late 1960s when serenading some young lady. I hadn't eaten one of these for years, but having tasted this recipe that one of my chefs has created, I might just try it again. Of course you can just start with loose scallops to save yourself the first 6 stages!

Fritto misto

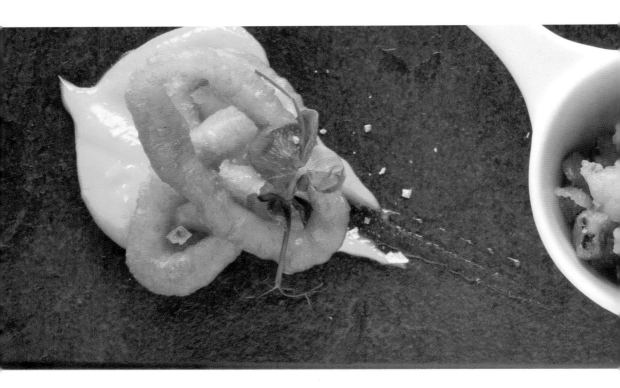

Ingredients

12 squid rings
40 cockles
4 fishcakes
8 king prawns

Tempura batter (cockle popcorn)
8oz plain flour
4oz cornflour
½ tsp baking powder
1 tsp bicarbonate of soda
200ml soda water

Salt and pepper batter (squid)
75g cornflour
90g plain four
2 ½ tbsp black peppercorns
2 tbsp Moldon sea salt
4 tbsp dried breadcrumbs
1 tsp bicarbonate of soda
1 pinch smoked paprika
3 egg whites

Piri Piri spice mix (prawns)
1 tsp salt (smoked)
½ tsp cinnamon powder
1 cardamon pod
½ tsp powdered sugar
½ tsp ground dry ginger
2 tsp paprika
1.5 tsp ground cayenne pepper or Piri Piri pepper
1 tsp chilli flakes
1 tsp oregano

Salmon fishcakes, see method on Page 172

350g floury potato, cut into chunks

350g salmon (about 3 fillets)

1 tsp English mustard

Zest of ½ lemon

1 heaped tbsp chopped parsley

1 heaped tbsp chopped dill

3 tbsp plain flour

1 egg, beaten

100g panko breadcrumbs

4 tbsp sunflower oil

Saffron aioli

4 tbsp hot water

1 tsp saffron threads

470ml canola oil or mild flavoured olive oil

4 egg yolk (preferably from a large, fresh farm egg)

4 tbsp freshly squeezed lemon juice

½ tsp minced garlic

1 tsp fine sea salt

RECIPE CONTINUES OVERLEAF

Method
(SERVES 4)

Tempura batter

1. Add ingredients together and whisk until smooth. Dip cockles in batter and fry.

Salt and pepper batter

1. Place salt and pepper in a hot pan and toast until fragrant, then blitz to a powder.

2. Place everything except the egg whites in a bowl and mix well. Dip the squid from the egg white to the flour then fry.

Saffron aioli

1. Soak the saffron threads in hot water for 10 minutes. Strain the saffron liquid into a wide-mouthed pint-size canning jar, pressing the threads to extract as much of the saffron essence as you can. Add the egg yolk, lemon juice and oil.

2. Using an immersion blender, blend just until the mixture thickens. Add salt and garlic to taste.

3. Cover and refrigerate for at least 1 hour to allow the flavours to meld.

This is a dish I put on the menu a couple of years ago and one which became very popular. Unfortunately, because it has several elements, we tend to now only serve it when we are quiet, but, it is a lovely combination of seafoods.

Chicken liver parfait and duck breast

Ingredients

Salt cure
100g table salt
100g white sugar
1tbsp black peppercorns
1 star anise
6 bay leaves

Duck
2 duck breasts
20g hickory smoking chips

Cherry gel for 'meat cherry'
150g cherry puree
20g glucose
30g po rt
20g cabernet sauvignon vinegar
3 sheets gelatine

Reduction
150ml port
150ml madeira
100ml brandy
5 peppercorns
½ banana shallot
2 bay leaves
1 ½ cloves of garlic
1 sprig of thyme

Chicken liver parfait
500g chicken livers (soaked in milk for 2 hours)
500g butter (clarified)
4 egg yolks (room temp)

RECIPE CONTINUES
OVERLEAF

Method
(SERVES 8-10)

Salt cure

1. Place all spice in a spice mill or food processor and blitz to a coarse powder. Mix all of the ingredients and store in an air tight container.

Duck

1. Trim the duck breasts of any excess fat, sprinkle over 2 tbsps of salt cure and set aside in the fridge for 4 hours. Wash well under cold water and place in a stove top smoker with around 20g of hickory smoking chips. Cook and smoke for 12 minutes until breast is medium rare. Place in a fridge to cool. Slice when needed.

Cherry gel for 'meat cherry'

1. Combine all of the ingredients in a saucepan, apart from the gelatine, and bring to the boil. Soak the gelatine leaves in cold water for 5 minutes, then squeeze out any excess water. Add to liquid then cool to room temperature. Pass liquid through a chinois.

2. Use the chicken liver parfait recipe to make the 'meat cherry'.

3. Whip the parfait in a food processor until smooth. Fill half-sphere moulds so that they are flush with the top. Use a piping bag if possible to prevent any air bubbles in the parfait when smoothing it off. Place in the freezer to set hard. However, do not allow to freeze as that can make the parfait grainy. Pop out the half-spheres and push together so the edges are flush. Smooth the join over with your finger so there is no visible join. Place on a cocktail stick and stick into polystyrene so they stand up, then return to the freezer to cool for one minute. Reheat the gel to 30C, dip the parfait in and return to the freezer to set. Repeat this process another 2 times to form a good layer of gel around each ball, make sure the gel stays at 30C for each dip or it will become cloudy when set around the cherry parfait. Once the final layer is set, place carefully in a tub on parchment. Don't stack or they may lose their shape. Serve with a real cherry stem in the hole where the cocktail stick was.

Reduction

1. Place all ingredients in a pan and reduce to form a syrup.

My parents used to make chicken liver pate, package them, and send them up to London to be on the shelves in various stores by the morning – this recipe is very similar to the one my mum made – gorgeous!

Wood pigeon, wood sorrel and toasted almond pesto, beetroot flavours

Ingredients

4 breasts of wood pigeon, shot removed

2 cups fresh wood sorrel

1 clove garlic

3 tbsp toasted almond flakes

1 pinch salt

¼ cup olive oil

2 medium beetroot

1 handful wood sorrel pesto to garnish

2 tsp red wine vinegar

Method
(SERVES 4)

Pesto

1.   Blend the sorrel, garlic, almonds and salt into a fine paste. Add the olive oil and blend again until smooth.

Beetroot

1.   Place one beetroot in a pan of cold water and boil until soft, for approximately 30 minutes. While still hot, peel the beetroot, add the vinegar to a blender and blend until smooth. Add a little hot water if too thick. Season and pass through a fine sieve.

2.   Peel and slice the other beetroot on a mandolin, as fine as possible, to 1mm. Lightly salt for 10 minutes then wash and pat dry. Fry at 180C in a deep fat fryer until they float for 2 minutes.

Pigeon

1.   Season and fry the pigeon breasts for 1-2 minutes, making sure they are still pink. Leave to rest, and serve sliced.

Well it's a wild bird, so can be a little on the tough side – but that's the nature of the dish. So my advice is to slice the breast into 4 to 6 slices so that it's easier to eat. Pigeon breast has a strong taste – I love it!

Pate de campagne

Ingredients

200g pork caul
200g pork loin
350g pork belly
50g chicken liver
1g thyme
7 bay leaves
1 onion
2 eggs
10g Sichuan pepper
100g baguette
50ml port
50ml Madiera
50ml white wine
Ground white pepper
7g salt
1g five spice

Method
(SERVES 6)

1.   Place the pork caul in cold water, changing the water a couple of times.

2.   Soak the baguette in all the alcohol.

3.   Mince the pork belly with the baguette and onion in a meat grinder.

4.   Chop the pork loin and mix with the minced meat and baguette. Add white pepper, salt, Sichuan pepper and whole eggs.

5.   In a ceramic terrine mould, place the bay leaves and half the thyme in the bottom then repeat on top once full. Spread the pork caul evenly. Place half of the mince mix in first then add the chicken liver and top with the rest of the mince mix, leaving an overflow space of 1cm from the top of the mould. Pack well and fold the pork caul over the top to seal.

6.   Place in a water bath and place in a pre-heated oven at 160C for 50 minutes. Once cooked, remove from the oven to cool. Refrigerate and allow to rest for 48 hours before serving.

I asked my French chef, Valentin, to come up with a pate de campagne and this is it. It reminds me of my time in France. You can make it as rough textured as you like – everywhere you would eat it, it would be different, a bit like a cassoulet, you never had exactly the same twice.

Scallop and belly pork with cauliflower textures

Ingredients

500g belly pork, see Page 114

4 scallops – corals removed

50g baby spinach

30g butter

4 baby carrots, scrubbed or peeled

1 small head of cauliflower

100ml vegetable oil

200ml milk

50ml white wine vinegar

1tsp caster sugar

1tsp pickling spices

Method
(SERVES 4)

1. Cut the belly pork into 4 fingers.

2. Scrape the fat off the pork skin and bake in the oven with the salt until cooked. Break up into pieces to garnish.

3. Heat the vinegar, caster sugar and pickling spices until sugar has dissolved. Leave to cool.

4. Break up the head of the cauliflower, choose 2 large florets to slice thinly. You will need 8 tidy slices from the middle section to pickle for 5 minutes, then drain off.

5. Prepare 8 florets and trim the stalks down to achieve little 'trees'. Blanche for 2 minutes. Fry the heads in oil, leaving the stalks white.

6. Chop down the remaining cauliflower into similar sized pieces and poach all the remaining cauliflower trim in the milk for 5-10 minutes then drain and blend until smooth, adding a little poaching liquid if necessary.

7. Blanch the spinach in boiling water for 30 seconds, drain, and squeeze out all the liquid. Mix with 10g melted butter and seasoning and form into 4 balls.

8. Cook the baby carrot and glaze with 10g melted butter.

9. Pan fry the belly pork in a little oil until crisp and golden, sear the scallops until ¾ cooked.

10. Arrange all the components on your plates.

11. Lastly, make the foam by bringing 100ml of the cauliflower milk and 10g butter to the boil. Use a hand held stick blender to make a froth, and spoon of the bubbles onto your dishes and serve immediately.

Scallops and belly pork are a classic combination, you can increase the size and serve as a main course.

Scallop, belly pork, carrot puree and chorizo

Ingredients

500g belly pork
100ml vegetable oil
1 star anise
1 sprig of thyme
4 large hand dived scallops (coral removed)
100g chorizo, diced small
25ml olive oil
2 large carrots, peeled
50g butter
50ml vegetable stock
Salt and pepper to taste

Method

(SERVES 4)

1. Lay the belly pork onto a roasting dish of similar size, add oil, anise and thyme and cover tightly with foil and slow bake for 2-3 hours. When tender, put onto a flat tray and press with another on top to make it flat whilst chilling. When totally cold, remove the skin and cut in to 8 tidy squares.

2. Pan fry the diced chorizo in the olive oil until slightly crispy.

3. Shred a small handful of carrot and deep fry until crispy.

4. Cut 4 tubes out of the carrot with an apple corer (or cut 4 large dice). Poach in the butter and vegetable stock, remove from the liquid. Chop the remaining carrot into similar sized pieces ad poach in the same liquid until well cooked. Strain and put the carrot into a food processor adding a little of the poaching liquid to obtain a smooth puree.

5. To assemble the dish, fry the belly pork in a little oil until crisp and golden and sear the scallops on a flat griddle or in a frying pan until coloured top and bottom, but only ¾ cooked.

6. Reheat the carrot and chorizo.

7. Put a swipe and dots of the carrot puree on the plate first, and arrange the pork, scallop, carrot tube, carrot crisps and chorizo.

Similar to the other scallop recipe and equally as delicious. We regularly feature these as starters and main courses. Very popular.

Avocado and prawn cocktail

Ingredients

Marie-rose sauce
3 dessert spoons of mayonnaise
Squirt of tomato sauce
½ tsp tomato paste
½ lemon – squeezed
Dash of paprika
Measure of brandy
Seasoning to taste

Stack
2 concassed tomato
16 large peeled prawns
2 gem leaves, shredded, but not too finely
2 lollo rosso leaves, shredded, but not too finely
Rocket
4 Greenland prawns, shell on
Few capers, squeezed out and deep fried for 30 seconds
1 avocado – peeled, stoned and sliced.
¼ cucumber – peeled, seeded and dried
50g crab meet mixed with 1 dessert spoon of mayonnaise and chopped tarragon
Marie-rose sauce

Method
(SERVES 4)

Marie-rose sauce

1. Mix all the ingredients together and taste. All tastes are different so adjust if you feel any one of the ingredients is too strong.

Stack

1. Mix the prawns with the marie-rose.

2. Mix the gem, lollo rosso, cucumber and sliced tomato. (To concass a tomato, simply pour over boiling water and when the skin begins to lift, pull it off. Leave the tomatoes to cool and chop them in half. Remove all the pips and thinly slice, or just chop.)

3. Layer up a 60mm ring with lettuce, prawn, sliced avocado and crab.

4. Garnish with the rocket, capers and Greenland prawn.

Avocado and prawn cocktail was one of the most popular starters of the 60s and 70s but it was quite basic looking, usually just a prawn cocktail sitting in half an avocado with a wedge of lemon. We have slightly revamped it, but still I can't get a chef to put it on a menu: 'Too easy and old hat' is what I get, but I love it, so here it is. If you really want to push the boat out, you can top it with slices of cooked lobster or a perfectly poached langoustine, or both!

MEAT

Duo of beef, fillet steak, cottage pie, Jerusalem artichoke, girolles

Ingredients

Cottage pie
500g pulled beef
1tbsp vegetable oil
1 onion, finely diced
2 cloves garlic, finely chopped
40ml Worcester sauce
1tsp tomato puree
1tsp flour
170ml beef stock
A few sprigs of thyme
50g swede, diced
1/2 carrot, diced
1 bay leaf

Fillet steak
4 x 150g fillet steak
Salt and pepper to taste
1 tsp vegetable oil

Tenderstem broccoli
3 sprigs Tenderstem broccoli
400ml water

Girolles
20g fresh girolles
50g welsh butter

Jerusalem artichoke
100g whole Jerusalem artichoke, peeled and trimmed
30g Welsh butter
Seasoning to taste

Method
(SERVES 4)

Cottage pie

1.   Fry the onion and garlic in a little oil until just coloured.

2.   Return the pulled beef to the pan, stir in the flour and tomato puree, then add the Worcester sauce.

3.   Add the beef stock and the bay leaf and fresh thyme. Bring to the boil.

4.   Blanch the diced carrot and swede for 6 minutes and add to the mix.

5.   Transfer the contents to a casserole dish and simmer it slowly in the oven with the lid on at 140C until the sauce is the right consistency.

Fillet steak

1.   Coat the fillet steak in oil, salt and pepper. Heat a non-stick frying pan until very hot (at flash point). Cook to your liking. Rest for 2/3 minutes.

Tenderstem broccoli

1.   Bring the water to a rolling boil, add the tenderstem, boil for 3 minutes, then strain. Serve immediately.

Girolles

1.   Brown the butter in a hot saucepan until golden brown, add the girolles and toss in the butter until coated. Remove from heat, but leave in the pan for a few minutes to cook through gently. Remove from the pan and drain on a paper towel. Keep warm until needed.

Jerusalem artichoke

1.   With the artichoke try to use pieces 1 inch-plus in size. Use an apple corer to cut out a tube lengthways, to leave you with a longer tube. Place in a small oven tray with butter and just a pinch of seasoning. Cover with tin foil and roast on 160C for 20-25 minutes until tender.

This dish combines a bit of finesse with some comfort food. It's not a dish we have done too often as customers seem to prefer one or the other and not the combination, but it works for me.

Duo of beef, seasonal vegetables

Ingredients

Shin bon bon
2 tbsp olive oil
1 shin of beef trimmed of fat
½ diced onion
3 cloves garlic, crushed
500ml beef stock
Sprigs of rosemary
Sprigs of thyme
2 bay leaves
Seasoning
200g breadcrumbs
2 eggs, beaten
100g plain flour

Cauliflower puree
1 medium cauliflower head, washed, peeled and roughly chopped
75ml double cream
25g butter
Seasoning
Lemon juice

Sirloin
1.8kg sirloin of beef, fat and sinew removed
2 cloves of garlic
Sprig of thyme
75g clarified butter
Seasoning

Method
(SERVES 8)

Shin bon bon

1. Heat the olive oil in a large frying pan and brown the beef shin for a few minutes. Transfer the shin to a large cast iron pan.

2. Add the onion and garlic and stir for a couple of minutes, then add the beef stock and herbs and season with salt and pepper. Bring to the boil and stir well. Transfer to a cast iron pan with the meat.

3. Cover the pan with foil and a lid and cook in the oven at 120C for 4 hours. When cooked, remove, cool and shred into balls.

4. Place the flour, egg and breadcrumbs into 3 separate bowls. Roll the bon bons in flour, then dip in egg and coat in breadcrumbs.

5. Heat 10cm of vegetable oil in a deep saucepan to 160C. Fry the bon bons in batches for 4-5 minutes until golden. Drain on a paper towel ready to plate up.

Cauliflower puree

1. Cover the cauliflower with water, add 1 tsp of salt. Boil until very soft, then strain through a fine sieve to extract as much liquid as possible.

2. Heat the cream and melt the butter.

3. Put the cream, butter and cauliflower in a blender and puree until completely smooth. Season to taste.

Sirloin

1. Cut the sirloin in half lengthways, wrap in cling film until resembling a large sausage. Place in fridge for a couple of hours to rest.

2. Cut the strips into equal medallions.

3. Fry the beef medallions in garlic, thyme and butter and season. Put in a warm place to rest for 5 minutes.

RECIPE CONTINUES OVERLEAF

Ingredients continued

Seasonal vegetables
Selection of seasonal baby vegetables
Seasoning
75g clarified butter

Jus
100ml Madeira
100ml port
250ml beef stock

Shallot onions
1 banana shallot per portion
50g clarified butter
Seasoning

Method continued
(SERVES 8)

Jus

1. Reduce the Madeira and port by ½ and add the beef stock and reduce until syrupy. Season.

Seasonal vegetables (whatever you choose)

1. Prep and peel the vegetables.

2. Blanch the vegetables in boiling water salted water. Toss the vegetables in clarified butter. Season and set aside ready to serve.

Shallot onions

1. Place the onion onto a baking try and season.

2. Put in an oven and roast until cooked through but still firm.

3. Trim away the first 2 layers of the onion to expose the tender core. Remove as much root as possible but keep the onion intact.

Another great combination dish. The trouble with these dishes is they do take a little love and times, but get it right and they are a joy to eat.

Fillet steak and tarragon lobster

Ingredients

Garlic butter

100g Welsh butter
1 tbsp parsley
1 clove garlic
1 tbsp chives
Half a tsp of salt

Fillet steak and tarragon lobster

800g fillet steak
Lobster tails or 8 prawns
4 baby leeks
8 baby carrots
1 packet mange tout
500ml orange juice
2 bay leaves
1 tbsp honey
1kg potatoes
50g butter
150ml double cream
100ml jus, see Page 156
Salt and pepper

Method
(SERVES 4)

Garlic butter

1. Soften the butter at room temperature. Mix all the ingredients together in a food processor until they are well combined and green. Roll into sausages in cling film and keep in fridge until needed.

Fillet steak and tarragon lobster

1. Season and sear the fillet steak on both ends and the sides until cooked to your liking. Rest for 5 minutes.

2. Prepare your lobster tail or peel the shell from your prawns and de-vein. Poach in tarragon butter for 3 minutes. Sear for 10 seconds each side in a hot pan.

3. Blanch the leek and mange tout in boiling water for 10 seconds. Char in a hot pan for 10 seconds each side.

4. Simmer the carrots in orange juice and honey for 10 seconds each side. Remove from the liquor and glaze in a hot pan with butter.

5. Boil the potatoes until just cooked. Press through a sieve to remove any lumps. Heat the cream, butter, salt and pepper and fold the hot cream into the hot mash until smooth.

6. Place the steak on a plate with 2 rounds of garlic butter – about ¼ inch each. Arrange the vegetables and lobster or prawns, and enjoy.

Surf and turf. Any fish can be used here if you can't get lobster; prawns or monkfish or similar will suffice, but of course for me it's lobster every time.

Beef kofta curry

Ingredients

Spice mix
Half a cinnamon stick
3tbsps fennel seed
6tbsps coriander seed
6tbsps cumin seed
2tbsps black onion seed
4tbsps black peppercorns
2tbsps garam masala
2tbsps turmeric
1 star anise
10 curry leaves
5 cardamom pods
5 cloves garlic

Base
3 inches fresh ginger
6 red onions
400ml vegetable oil
15 garlic cloves
(Blend all the above
together)
4tbsps tomato puree
1kg chopped tomatoes
1.2ltrs water

Kofta
1kg beef mince
6 cloves of garlic
30g chopped coriander
1tbsp ground coriander
½ tbsp ground cumin
½ tbsp ground black
pepper
½ tbsp salt

Fragrant rice
1tbsp coriander seed
5 cardamom
4 star anise
1tbsp cumin seed
5 bay leaves
Salt
350g basmati rice

Method
(SERVES 4-6)

Spice mix

1.   Toast and blend together in a mixer or pestle & mortar.

Kofta

1.   Combine the ingredients and shape into Koftas.

Base

1.   Place a heavy-based pan on the heat. Now heat to flash point/ smoking.

2.   Firstly, add the first batch of base ingredients – ginger, onions, oil and garlic – and fry for 6/7 minutes. Now add the spice mix and fry for another 5/6 minutes.

3.   Once well fried, add the tomato puree, chopped tomatoes and water and simmer for 1 hour.

4.   Add the Kofta to the sauce and cook for a further 30 minutes until the meat is cooked.

5.   Serve and refrigerate.

Fragrant rice

1.   Doubling the amounts in the recipe will give you enough rice to serve 8-10 people.

2.   Put a large pan of water on a high heat and add the spices and salt. Boil for about 7-8 minutes to allow the water to take on the spice flavours. Strain the loose spices out with a sieve before adding the rice. Rinse the rice in a colander under running water for about 1 minute, or until the water runs clear (this will stop the grains sticking together later).

3.   Add the rice to the boiling water and wait for the grains to start dancing around. From that point, boil for 5-6 minutes.

4.   Remove from the heat and if you're ready, serve immediately. If not, place under a cold tap to refresh with the water running slowly so the rice doesn't escape from the pan with the overflowing water. Strain in a colander once cold.

I do have the original beef kofta curry that Mrs Pringle in the early 60s served out to admiring customers at the 'Hat and Feather', but this isn't it. Why not? Because the recipe she gave me most surely wasn't. So from memory I have tried to recreate the dish and it tastes much nearer to what I remember.

Chilli beef platter

Ingredients

Beef brisket

1kg beef brisket, cut in to
1 inch cubes

2tbsps olive oil

1 small chopped onion

2 large garlic cloves,
minced

1/2tsp chilli powder

1tsp red pepper flakes,
crushed

1tsp cayenne pepper, or
to taste

2tsp ground cumin

1 green pepper, seeded
and diced

1 bay leaf

800g tomatoes, chopped
with their liquid

Salt and pepper to taste

2tbsps strong coffee

100g canned kidney beans

2tsp chopped basil leaves

Saffron Rice

Sea salt

1/2tsp turmeric

1tsp saffron

350g basmati rice

Method
(SERVES 4-6)

Brisket

1. Pat the brisket cubes dry with paper towels.

2. Heat the oil in a very large heavy based pot and quickly brown the meat, in batches, on all sides. Transfer the brisket to a separate bowl and set aside. Saute the onion and garlic in the same oil over a medium heat until limp, but not brown (about 8-10 minutes). Add the chilli powder, pepper flakes, cayenne pepper and cumin and saute for 1 minute. Add the green peppers, bay leaf, tomatoes with their juice, the reserved meat, 1tsp of salt and ½ tsp pepper and bring to a boil. Reduce the heat, cover the pot with a tight fitting lid and simmer for 2 ½ hours, stirring occasionally. Taste and season with salt to taste. Add the coffee, cover the pot and simmer for 1 more hour.

3. Add the kidney beans and basil and warm through. Transfer the chilli to a large serving bowl and serve with sour cream, grated cheddar, diced tomato, tortilla chips and guacamole.

Saffron rice

1. Doubling the amounts will give you enough to serve 8-12 people.

2. Put a large pan of water on a heat and bring to the boil and add the saffron, turmeric and salt, boil for 5 minutes to allow to infuse. Rinse the rice in a colander under running water and wait for the grains to start dancing around. From that point, boil for 5-6 minutes.

3. Drain the rice in a colander, remove from the heat and if you're ready, serve. If not, lay out on a flat tray in a thin layer so it cools quickly, use a fridge to rapid cool if you have space.

RECIPE CONTINUES OVERLEAF

Ingredients

Sour cream
100ml double cream
Juice from 1 lemon
1 tsp finely chopped chives
Pinch of salt

Pickled vegetables
Pickling juice
150ml white wine vinegar
2 tsps pickling spices
2tsps sugar

Vegetables
4 florets cauliflower broken
into small pieces
2 radishes – thinly sliced
1 banana shallot – thinly
sliced
1 medium carrot cut in to
ribbons

Tortilla wraps
2 tortilla wraps
1tsp smoked paprika
Salt and pepper

Method

Sour cream

1. Whisk together all the ingredients until firm, make 4 large roche's with a tablespoon.

Pickled vegetables/Pickling juice

1. Mix all the ingredients together and bring to the boil to dissolve the sugar. Leave to cool and strain.

Vegetables

1. Steep the vegetables in the pickle overnight, drain off and put into 4 small jars.

Tortilla wraps

1. Cut the wraps into 8 segments each, deep fry until crisp. Dust with smoked paprika, salt and pepper.

Heart-warming cold evening supper – it is a case of chucking all the ingredients into a big pot and forgetting about it for a while – not that hard to do but very rewarding with bags of flavour.

Sussex beef pie

Ingredients

Filling
2kg diced rump
500ml Guinness
500ml ale
1.5ltrs beef stock
3 onions – diced
6 field mushrooms, halved and sliced
4 cloves garlic, finely chopped
50g demerara sugar
2 large sprigs of thyme – stalks removed
Salt and pepper for seasoning
Vegetable oil

Short crust pastry
500g plain flour
250g diced cold butter
Pinch of salt
2 eggs & 2tbsp water beaten together

Method
(SERVES 6)

Filling

1. Batch fry diced beef in very hot frying pans with a little oil to colour and seal the edges, seasoning lightly as you go.

2. Put into a large saucepan and repeat with onions, mushrooms and garlic. De-glaze the pan with the Guinness and ale.

3. Add the thyme, demerara and half the stock to the saucepan and bring to a gentle simmer. Cook until the meat is tender (approximately 1 ½ - 2 hours) adding more stock if required (this is normally thick enough but if you want a thicker sauce just add 2 tablespoons of cornflour mixed with a little water). Allow to cool.

Pastry

1. Put the flour, butter and salt into a food processor and pulse for 5 seconds, add the eggs and water and pulse for a further 5 seconds.

2. Turn onto a work surface and gently bring it together and form into a ball. Wrap in cling film and allow to rest for 20 minutes.

3. Divide pastry into 9 equal pieces and cut 3 of the pieces in half, these will be the lids.

4. Lightly butter 6 individual pie dishes.

5. Roll out one of the larger pieces of pastry to line the dish, overhanging slightly. Fill the pie dish 4/5ths full with the filling and wet the rim with water.

6. Roll out the smaller pastry piece and place on top and crimp and trim, repeat 5 more times.

7. Any filling left over, depending on the size of your pie dishes, can be eaten with rice.

Any pie done in this format – chicken, ham and mushroom etc is a winner. Much better than just putting a lid on a casserole mix which so often happens.

Tournedos Rossini

Ingredients

Ingredients
4 x 200g fillet steaks
4 rounds of thick cut bread
50ml olive oil
150g chicken liver parfait,
see Page 104
12 button mushrooms,
turned
75g butter
8 banana shallots
100ml vegetable oil
Sprig of thyme
Red wine jus, see Page 164
Salt and pepper to taste

Method
(SERVES 4)

1.   Heat 25ml of olive oil and 25g of butter in a frying pan until
it stops foaming. Fry the bead rounds on both sides until an
even colour is achieved. Drain on kitchen paper and keep warm.

2.   Confit the shallots whole, skin on, with vegetable oil and
thyme for 15 minutes. Halve lengthways and sear them, side
down until the edges brown. Remove and keep warm.

3.   Lightly fry the mushrooms in 25g butter, drain and keep
warm.

4.   Heat a heavy based frying pan until very hot, and add the
remaining olive oil. Cook the fillets to your liking. (Anything
more than rare is sacrilege!!)

5.   Whilst finishing the steaks, add the butter and coat until
nut brown, remove from the pan and leave to rest for 3 minutes.

6.   To assemble the dish, divide the parfait between the 4
steaks and grill for 20 seconds to heat the plate. Place a fillet on
the bead round. Garnish the plate with the mushrooms, cut the
root off the shallots and discard the skins. Arrange around the
fillet and drizzle some red wine jus around the plate.

In the early years you would put the pate on
the crouton, the mushroom on the top and
pour the red wine jus over – The Leigh Arms in
Prestbury. This takes me back to my youth!'

Venison duo

Ingredients

330g venison haunch meat
1 bay leaf
1 clove of garlic
1 sprig of rosemary
1 sprig of thyme
2 juniper berries
6 tbsp butter
1 peeled shallot
200g peeled and grated potato
1/2 tsp picked thyme
100g flour
1 egg
200ml milk
200g panko bread crumbs
800g venison loin
1 large or 2 small celeriac
8 baby carrots
200g kale
2 Maris piper potatos
200ml red wine
200ml chicken stock
50ml single cream

A dish we have on our menu at present and one the AA inspector was very happy with on his recent visit when confirming our 2 AA Rosette.

Method
(SERVES 4)

1. First make the croquette. Braise the meat in a tight-fitting dish or a roasting bag. Preheat the oven to 140C. Add the venison haunch, bay leaf, garlic, rosemary, thyme sprig, 50ml of the red wine, juniper and 1tbsp of the butter. Braise for 6 hours.

2. Grate the potato and squeeze out any excess moisture with a tea towel, dice the shallot.

3. Soften the shallot in 1tbsp of the butter, add the grated potato and continue to cook until the potato is just cooked. Set aside.

4. Remove any sinew from the venison and shred the meat slightly. Strain and reduce any braising juices. Mix the potato, jus, venison meat and the picked thyme leaves together by hand until the mixture binds together.

5. Once the mixture has cooled weigh out into 50g portions and shape into long cylinders (croquettes). Chill these before dusting with flour, dip in egg wash and panko bread crumbs, now place the finished croquettes in the fridge.

6. Trim any sinew from the venison loin and wrap tightly in cling film several times, cut into equal portions and sear both ends, season with salt and pepper.

7. With half of your celeriac, peel and trim until it's as square as possible. Cut into neat squares or rectangles, usually 8 from a medium celeriac. Gently fry in a little oil on each side, season and add the remaining 4tbsp of butter and chicken stock until the celeriac is just covered. Simmer on both sides until soft, usually about 15 minutes. Set aside to cool

8. With the rest of the celeriac peel and dice into cubes and cover with boiling water, simmer until the celeriac is soft. Blend with some of the liquid and the cream until totally smooth. Season and set aside to cool.

9. Clean the kale and baby carrots in cold water and blanch the carrots until they are nearly cooked, with a firm bite.

10. Deglaze all the venison flavour from all the pans and bowls. Set that gently simmering. Reduce until thickened; it may need a sprinkle of sugar if it's bitter.

11. Peel the Maris piper potato and set the mandolin slicer to have the crinkle cutter sticking out at 3mm. Now push the potato through the slicer and rotate the potato on its cut edge by 90 degrees either way. Repeat the process with a little adjusting of the blade depth to get the perfect gaufrette potato, place all the best slices in cold water.

12. To serve the dish you will need your fryer hot at 180C, a pan of boiling salted water and a hot frying pan.

13. Place the croquettes and the gaufrette chips in the fryer until crisp and golden. Sear the remaining sides of the venison fillet in the frying pan until about medium rare. Heat the venison red wine jus, celeriac puree and celeriac fondant. Drop the kale and carrots into boiling water for a minute.

14. Now arrange the elements of the dish as you like on the plate.

Coda alla vaccinara

Ingredients

1 oxtail, jointed
2 onions
2 sticks celery
1 carrot
4 slices back bacon
3 cloves garlic
2 bay leaves
1 sprig of thyme
1 tin chopped plum tomatoes
500ml chicken stock
500ml red wine
50g toasted pinenuts
50g sultanas
1 tbsp chopped parsley
Seasoning to taste

Method
(SERVES 4)

1. Finely chop the onions, celery, carrot, bacon and garlic. Remove the thyme from the stalks and chop.

2. Fry off the oxtail in oil until coloured on all sides then remove from frying pan. Fry off the finely chopped vegetables and bacon until soft, then add to the oxtail in a heavy-based saucepan or oven proof dish. Add the bay leaves, thyme, tomatoes, stock and wine. Cook gently for 3-4 hours or until oxtail can be pulled off the bone. Add the pine nuts, sultanas, parsley and seasoning and cook for another 15 minutes.

This dish was one my sister used to put on her menu at David's place in the 1970s – I loved it, so we stole it. Oxtail is one of my favourite meats, and in the old days it was very cheap. If you bought a couple of steaks from a butcher, he would probably give you the oxtail – it's a shame that's no longer the case!

Pork fillet, Danish style

Ingredients

3 pork fillets, trimmed and battered flat
1 mug prunes
8 apple, peeled and chopped
Dash of Calvados
1½ onions, finely diced
Large measure of Calvados
300ml chicken stock
Medium glass white wine
Chopped sprig of sage
4 bay leaves
Salt and pepper to season
Large spoon of cream
Sunflower oil
Flour

Method
(SERVES 6)

1. Lay the fillets on a board. Trim and flatten them out so that they are only ½ inch thick. You will need to make at least 2 incisions into the fillet so that you can flatten it. Place prunes and sliced apple onto the first fillet. Season, and repeat with another fillet, laying the third on top.

2. Tie up the meat like a large sausage.

3. Place the large pork sausage in a frying pan and roll around to brown all over. Flame in the Calvados and remove to an oven-proof dish.

4. Add the onion to the oil and sauté until opaque then stir in the flour. You want to end up with a roux two-thirds the size of a golf ball.

5. Slowly add the hot stock and the wine, until you have a fair amount of sauce, using more of each if necessary.

6. Add the sauce with the sage, the rest of the apples, prunes, bay leaves and season to taste.

7. Pop on the lid, put in a medium hot oven and leave for 30 minutes and then check. You want the middle of the fillet to be just cooked – too far and it can be a dry.

8. Finally, take out the 'sausage' and add a little cream to the sauce. Check for consistency and seasoning.

9. Sauté a few apple rings, slice the pork, pour the sauce over and pop a few rings on the top – et voila!!

An early dish at the Hat and Feather, but a popular one. Ideal for entertaining as it is all done beforehand, and all you have to do is put a few glazed apple rings on it. A dish that you might have been suspicious about (prunes) but that will delight your guests.

Rack of spring lamb and cockle and leek gratin

Ingredients

Cockle and leek gratin,
see Page 182

Rack of spring lamb
French trim rack of lamb
(I recommend allowing
a 3-bone segment per
person)

Garnish
Broad beans (blanched
and shelled)
Garden peas (blanched)
Asparagus (blanched)
Samphire (blanched)
Sea rosemary
Wild garlic
New potatoes (boiled)
Laverbread (warmed
through in a pan)
Olive oil
Lemon juice

Method
(SERVES 4)

Rack of spring lamb

1.   Season the lamb with salt and pepper. Bring a frying pan to a high heat and then fry the lamb on all sides until well-sealed and brown. Transfer the lamb into a baking dish and continue to cook in the oven for a further 10 minutes at 170C.

2.   Remove the lamb from the oven and allow a further 5 minutes for the lamb to rest. Keep the roasting juices. Slice lamb into chops before serving.

Garnish

1.   Place 2 or 3 new potatoes on each plate along with 2tsp of laverbread. Arrange the lamb chops over the potatoes and then the beans, peas, asparagus and samphire. Garnish with wild garlic leaves and sea rosemary and place cockle gratin on plate.

2.   Make a quick dressing by whisking together the roasting juices from the lamb with olive oil, lemon juice, salt and pepper. Spoon over the lamb and serve.

Wales and lamb: We have so much lovely lamb. Pick the right time of year, find a good honest butcher, there are still a few, and you will have a joyous meal made even more Welsh with the cockle and leek gratin.

Salt marsh lamb & scallops

Ingredients

Sea beet potato cake

3 egg yolks

4 egg whites

375g cold mashed potato

1tbs sea salt flakes

1/2tbs cracked black pepper

110g sea beet fine sliced, or spinach will work fine if you don't live near the sea

3tbs soft butter

Everything else

2 trimmed salt marsh lamb rump

1 shoulder of salt marsh, boned and rolled

8 hand dived scallops

1 pomegranate

1 radicchio lettuce

200ml lamb or veal jus

4 spring onions

2tbs fresh mint

RECIPE CONTINUES OVERLEAF

Method
(SERVES 4)

Sea beet potato cake

1. Mix the egg yolk and mashed potato to a smooth puree, add the salt, pepper, butter, seabeet or spinach. Fold till well mixed.

2. Whip the egg whites till soft peaks, stir in half the egg whites and gently fold in the rest. Place in a 20x20cm baking tray.

3. Bake for 25-30 minutes on 175°C in a fan-assisted oven.

4. Once cooled, cut into circles or squares as desired.

Lamb shoulder

1. In a hot oven roast the seasoned lamb in a tray for 15 minutes, until browned all over.

2. Cover half way up the side of the lamb with water.

3. Turn the oven down to 140°C.

4. Cover the lamb and return to the oven for at least 4 hours or until soft like butter.

5. Once slightly cooled remove the string and roll the lamb in heavy duty cling film to form a cylinder.

6. Cool in the fridge until needed.

Lamb rump

1. Season the rumps all over and in a hot frying pan. Seal on all sides.

2. Place in a 170°C fan oven for 10-15 minutes or as you like it.

3. Put in a warm place to rest for 6 minutes.

Scallops

1. Prepare the scallops by removing any roe, or skirt

2. Season lightly with salt and pepper.

3. In a hot frying pan, cook the scallops for 1 minute on each side.

4. Put in a warm place to rest.

Plating up

1. Slice the lamb shoulder into 3cm thick discs, fry for 3 minutes each side in a medium hot pan.

2. Place the cut potato cakes in the oven to warm through.

3. Slice the radicchio.

4. Cut the pomegranate in half and pick the fruit.

5. Finely slice the mint and cut the spring onions into 2cm lengths.

6. Place all the items on the plate as desired, a line of the items through the middle of the plate works nicely.

7. Pour a little jus over the lamb and scallops.

Another great Welsh lamb dish involving the best of Wales.

Devilled lamb kidneys

Ingredients

8 very fresh lamb kidneys cut in half (remove white core)

2 shallots finely diced

100ml brandy

6 drops Worcester Sauce

1 tbsp reduced beef stock

1 tbsp Dijon mustard

1 large red chilli de-seeded and finely diced

100ml double cream

Pinch sea salt

Pinch pepper

1 healthy sprig rosemary

1 punnet of rocket leaves

4 rounds of thick cut bread

25g butter

25ml oil

Method
(SERVES 4 AS A STARTER OR 2 AS A MAIN)

1. In a hot frying pan add a little oil and place the kidneys in it, sliced-side down. Wait 2 minutes before flipping them. Once browned all over, reduce the heat to medium and add the shallots. Fry for one minute then add the brandy flame to burn off the alcohol.

2. Add the Worcester Sauce, Dijon, beef stock and chilli. Bash the rosemary with a rolling pin and add that too.

3. Add the cream and reduce. Remove the kidneys if they look like they will overcook. Season with salt and pepper to taste.

4. Heat the butter and oil in a large frying pan. Fry the bread rounds until golden on both sides then drain on kitchen paper. Place on a plate, and top with the kidneys and sauce.

5. Serve with a few leaves of rocket.

This is a dish from the early years. Offal is not so prevalent on menus today, basically because environmental health wants us to overcook it to make it safe. In my opinion it's a shame, but health is health and the law is the law – but I love pink offal, and when cooking for myself I always cook it so!

Lamb's liver, bacon and sage sauce, onion rings

Ingredients

Lamb's liver

1kg lamb's liver –
membrane and large veins
removed

Green beans and sage
leaves (optional)

1 cup seasoned flour

50g butter

Mashed potato

1kg Maris Piper or Rooster
potatoes – peeled

2oz butter

100ml cream

Bacon and sage sauce

1 onion – finely diced

10 rashers smoked streaky
bacon cut into lardons

10 sage leaves

500ml double cream

200ml chicken stock (2tsp
chicken bouillon)

Onion rings

1 onion – cut into rings

4oz plain flour

3oz cornflour

¼ tsp bicarbonate soda

¼ tsp baking powder

250ml soda water

Method
(SERVES 4)

Lamb's liver

1. Slice the liver across the lobe for large scallops, approximately 5mm thick.

2. Heat a heavy based frying pan until very hot, add a knob of butter and melt.

3. Pass slivers of liver through the seasoned flour and shake off the excess. Cook for approximately 30 seconds each side depending on how well done you want your liver.

Mashed potato

1. Boil potatoes until just cooked, strain for 5 minutes.

2. Pass through a sieve for a fine mash (or use a ricer).

3. Boil the cream and butter together, add the potato and work with a spatula until glossy. Season to taste.

Bacon and sage sauce

1. Sweat the onions until translucent.

2. Fry the lardons separately until golden brown. Drain and add to the onions.

3. Add the cream and chicken stock along with finely chopped sage.

4. Simmer for 5 minutes or until slightly reduced.

Onion rings

1. Pass the onion rings through seasoned flour then into batter and finally into the fryer. Cook until golden on each side.

Assembly

1. Spoon the mash onto plates, top with liver and add the onion rings. Coat with sauce.

2. Serve with green beans and sage leaves (optional).

This used to be our most popular lunch dish – but environmental health pulled us up for not cooking it well done in order to reach the required 'safe' temperature, so, as I hate it to be cooked any more than medium, we have had to take it off. A shame really!

Lamb rump, feta bon bon & salsa verde jus

Ingredients

4 x 250g lamb rumps

Lamb rump marinade
Thyme and rosemary, 3 sprigs
each
3 sprigs garlic
200ml olive oil

Feta bon bon
2 sprigs thyme
Zest of 1 lemon
200g feta
Cream
Panko breadcrumbs
1 beaten egg

Potato fondant
200g butter
4 potatoes, peeled, cut into
squares
3 cloves garlic
2 sprigs thyme
100ml lamb stock

Salsa Verde	**Jus**	**Beetroot puree**
Handful of each: mint, basil, parsley, capers	1kg lamb trimmings	500g roast beetroot, skin removed
1 clove garlic, diced	½ kg chicken wings	100g butter
2tsps white wine vinegar	2ltrs water	15ml balsamic vinegar
8tbsps olive oil	½ bottle red wine	40ml water
	4 celery sticks	Salt to taste
	4 carrots	
	8 onions	
	2 bay leaves	
	2 star anise	RECIPE CONTINUES OVERLEAF

Method
(SERVES 4)

Lamb rump marinade

1.   Add all the ingredients into a blender and blitz. Pour over the lamb rumps and leave to marinade for 12 hours. Remove from the marinade and sear on all sides. Cook in oven for 10 – 20 minutes on 180C, depends on how you like your lamb cooked.

Feta bon bon

1.   Add feta, zest of lemon and leaves of thyme to a blender, blitz to form a paste adding a splash of cream to bind. Leave to set in the fridge. Once firm, form into balls. Roll in flour and dip in beaten egg and coat with Panko breadcrumbs, deep fry until golden.

Potato fondant

1.   Heat butter in a pan until foaming. Add the potato and fry until golden brown. Turn over, and repeat. Add the garlic and thyme to the pan then pour in the lamb stock to cover. Continue cooking on a low to medium heat until cooked through. Finish with salt and pepper.

Salsa verde

1.   Chop garlic, then add to blender with herbs, capers and vinegar. Pour in oil and pulse to a medium/coarse texture, then season to taste.

Jus

1.   Roast the chicken wings and lamb trimmings at 200C until brown. Roast the carrots, onion and celery in a separate tray. Once cooked, transfer meat and roast vegetables into a saucepan and add remaining ingredients. Cook until reduced by two thirds. To make the sauce, mix the jus and salsa verde at 50/50 ratio.

Beetroot puree

1.   Roast fresh beetroot on 140C for 2 hours, making sure it's well covered in a tray with tin foil. Once cooked remove skin and cut into half inch cubes. Add all ingredients together in a deep pan and cook for 10-15 minutes, then pour into a food processor and blitz for 5 minutes until smooth and silky. Pass through a fine sieve and season to taste.

Any Welsh lamb in season, marsh lamb preferably, done this way is just the best – I love all the additions to the main event – divine!

Coq au vin

Ingredients

Saffron oil/butter

1 free range chicken – jointed into 8

16 button onions/shallots

6 thick bacon rashers cut in to lardons

1 pt chicken stock

Medium glass of red wine

20 button mushrooms

3 bay leaf

Measure of brandy

Flour

Salt and pepper

Finely chopped clove of garlic (optional)

Method
(SERVES 4)

1. Coat the chicken joints in seasoned flour and place in a large frying pan containing a small knob of butter. Add a good splash of oil. Fry off the joints until they begin to brown, then flame the joints over the heat with the brandy.

2. Remove the chicken joints and set aside. Add lardons, onions, mushrooms and garlic. Stir until they begin to colour (5 minutes approximately), add a little more flour if it's too oily.

3. Slowly pour in half the hot chicken stock and stir to ensure no lumps, then slowly add the red wine and bay leaves. Add the rest of the stock to create a thin-ish sauce – more stock may be required.

4. Season to taste, add the chopped parsley and add the chicken back into the dish. Bring to the boil and place in an oven proof dish.

5. With the lid on, cook in a medium–hot oven for approximately 50 minutes.

I remember this in the 1950s. Mum, if having a dinner party, would often cook this dish. Of course she would use burgundy to cook with and probably have a glass on the side for herself, a must for any chef I would say! Cooked properly it's still delicious eating!

Chicken supreme Elizabeth

Ingredients

Chicken

2 chicken supreme with knuckle and skin on

2tbs flour

1tbsp sea salt flakes

1tbsp cracked black pepper

1tbsp dried mushroom powder

1tbsp cayenne pepper

2tbsps oil

Sauce

100ml medium white wine

25ml white wine vinegar

40g butter

100ml chicken stock

20g mushroom powder

300g field or button mushrooms

400ml whole milk

100ml double cream

4 asparagus spears

1 large vine tomato

Method
(SERVES 4)

1. To make the mushroom powder, use 200g peelings from field mushrooms or finely slice some button mushrooms. Place on a radiator or warm place to dry. When fully dried out, blitz.

Chicken

1. In a bowl, mix all of the dry ingredients and prepare your chicken supreme. Clean the edges and remove the meat form the bone (optional).

2. Rub the dry mix all over the chicken. Add the oil to a medium hot frying pan then carefully brown the chicken supremes.

3. When nicely browned, set the chicken aside.

Sauce

1. Clean the pan and set back on the heat. Half some and dice the rest of the mushrooms and fry in a little oil. Once they have some colour, add the wine, vinegar and butter. Reduce by half then stir in the mushroom powder and chicken stock. Bring to the boil then add the milk and cream. Once the sauce has thickened slightly, pour into two oval dishes approx 8 inches long.

2. In a pan of boiling salted water, blanch the asparagus spears for 15 seconds then refresh in ice. Cut into 3cm lengths and arrange around the edge of the two dishes, sprinkle the tomato over the sauce and place the chicken supreme in the middle of each dish.

3. Bake in a pre-heated oven for 25-30 minutes at 175°C in a fan-assisted oven or 190°C in a conventional oven.

A dish from the early years, a lovely way to eat chicken.

Thai green chicken curry

Ingredients

For the paste
1 bunch of spring onions
2 inches of fresh ginger
6 cloves of garlic
10 green chillies
2 green peppers
1tbsp shrimp paste

Spices
2tbsp coriander seeds
1tbsp cumin seeds
2tsp cardamom pods
1tsp ground turmeric

To finish
3 lemongrass
4 kaffir lime leaves
5 chicken breasts
2 tbsp fish sauce
25g palm sugar
1 lime juice
1 can of coconut milk
Handful of fresh coriander
Salt

Method
(SERVES 4)

1.   Toast the spices gently in a hot pan before grinding in a spice mill.

2.   Blend all the paste ingredients thoroughly and combine with spices.

3.   In a large pre-heated saucepan fry the diced chicken, lemongrass and lime leaves until the chicken is sealed (5 minutes).

4.   Add the paste and continue to fry for a further 5 minutes, stirring regularly.

5.   Add the coconut milk and continue to cook for a further 5 minutes.

6.   Reduce the heat and finish the curry with palm sugar, fish sauce, lime juice, coriander and salt to taste.

This is a lovely version of the dish. One of my favourite curries. Mind you, find me a curry I don't like! The hotter the better for me!

Duck confit

Ingredients

Simple red wine jus
2 chopped shallots
175ml port
175ml red wine
1 sprig rosemary
1 bay leaf
800ml good beef stock
Salt to taste
2tbs butter

Duck confit
6 duck legs
Salt cure, see Page 104
1.5ltr oil or duck fat
4 star anise
4 bay leaves
10 pepper corns
6 cloves of garlic
2 sprigs of thyme

Creamed savoy and bacon
300ml double cream
30g bacon lardons
½ savoy cabbage – stems removed and finely shredded
Salt and pepper to taste

Mashed potato
1kg red rooster potatoes, peeled and diced into 2 inch pieces
2.5lt water
200ml double cream
150g welsh butter
Salt and pepper to taste

Method
(SERVES 6)

Simple red wine jus

1. Panfry shallots to caramelise.

2. Add port, wine and herbs then reduce to half.

3. Add stock and reduce by half.

4. Strain through a sieve and bring back to the boil and reduce until syrupy. When done, remove from the heat and add butter, then season to taste.

Duck confit

1. Lay the duck legs on a tray and salt well. Leave in the fridge for 6 hours. Once ready, wash well under cold water and dry. Lay the duck legs in a deep tray (2.5 inches deep). Place all the ingredients into the tray over the duck legs and cover well with baking parchment and tin foil. Heat the oven to 110C and the cook duck legs for 6-7 hours until soft. Put the tray somewhere cold or in the fridge if it fits. Once cold, remove from the tray when needed and leave in the fat to preserve the freshness.

Creamed savoy and bacon

1. For the bacon lardons, use cured smoked streaky bacon and slice thinly into lardons. Fry in a pan with oil until crisp and caramelised, then strain through a sieve to remove any excess fat and oil.

2. Pour double cream into a deep saucepan with the bacon lardons and gently boil on a low heat, stirring every few minutes to stop it sticking to the bottom. Remove from the heat when the sauce is sticky and thick.

3. Blanch the savoy in boiling water for 2 minutes until softened a little. Add the creamy bacon to the savoy in a different pan and cook together for a further 2/3 minutes and season to taste.

Mashed potato

1. Add 1 tsp of salt to water in a deep pan and bring to the boil. Once boiling, add the potatoes and boil for 20/25 minutes until tender. Strain through a colander and leave air dry for 5 minutes until fluffy. Once dry, pass through a drum sieve and then repeat once more. Place back into a deep pan and place back on a low heat. Add the cream and butter and mix well until well combined. Season to taste and serve.

I love duck confit on a French cassoulet – beans, tomatoes, pork belly, garlic and sausage – but when we serve it like that it just doesn't sell, such a pity. Serve it traditionally on mash with cabbage and it flies out – so here it is.

FISH

Fish pie

Ingredients

250g smoked haddock
375g salmon
125g chopped smoked salmon
220g prawns
2 spring onions
300ml fish stock
1tbsp chopped parsley
150ml white wine
½ onion diced
1 lemon squeezed
100g button mushrooms halved
Few finely chopped chives
Dash of oil
50g butter
50g plain flour
50ml single cream
Salt and pepper

Method
(SERVES 4)

1. Lightly fry the onions and mushrooms then add the flour.

2. Stir to create a light roux, then add the stock slowly and then the wine.

3. Add in the spring onions, parsley and chives and bring to the boil.

4. Add in the salmon, haddock, smoked salmon, prawns, lemon and seasoning.

5. Take off the stove and portion into your dishes.

6. Add mashed potato onto the top (make it how you wish). Add a bit of single cream and butter and season well. Using a fork, spread it or use a piping bag – either way it's easier if the pie is cool.

7. Grate a little mature cheddar onto the potato and cook in a warm to hot oven for 25 minutes, or until going brown on the top.

This is a dish you can add any fish to – monkfish, mussels or even lobster. It's real comfort food and cooked in this way is a great eat! We still serve this, but have modernised the style of how it is served – we put all the fish, hot, in an open soup bowl or pasta dish – put 2 quenelles of mash on the top and sprinkle a cheesy crumb onto the mash!

Tempura battered cod

Ingredients

Cod
4 fillets

Tempura batter
8oz plain flour
4oz corn flour
½ tsp baking powder
1 tsp bicarbonate of soda
200ml soda water

Tartare sauce
3 egg yolks
1 tsp English mustard
1 tsp white wine vinegar
250ml rapeseed oil
½ tsp chopped fresh chives
½ tsp chopped fresh chervil
½ tsp chopped fresh parsley
3 chopped gherkins
Salt and pepper
3 tsp chopped capers
Small squeeze lemon juice

Method
(SERVES 4)

Tempura batter

1.   Add the ingredients together and whisk.

2.   Coat the cod in the batter and deep fry until done.

Tartare sauce

1.   Start by making the mayonnaise. Whisk the egg yolk, vinegar and mustard together in a bowl until well combined. Slowly add the rapeseed oil in a steady stream while continuing to whisk until emulsified.

2.   Finely dice the gherkins and add to the mayonnaise along with the capers and chopped herbs. Taste and adjust the seasoning with salt and pepper as necessary.

I asked the AA inspector if fish and chips could sit on a 2 rosette menu – she replied – 'only if it's an exceptionally good one'. Well, this is. Couple fresh fish in a light tempura batter with triple cooked chips (ensure the oil is fresh and clean), and you have the perfect fish and chips.

Salmon fishcake

Ingredients

Chilli and red pepper jam

4 red pepper, deseeded and roughly chopped

5 red chilies

2cm fresh root ginger, peeled and roughly chopped

4 garlic cloves, peeled

200g cherry tomatoes

375g golden caster sugar

125ml red wine vinegar

Salmon Fishcakes

250g floury potato, cut into chunks cut – pipers or roosters

350g salmon skinless (about 3 fillets)

1 tsp English mustard

Zest of ½ lemon

1 heaped tbsp chopped parsley

1 heaped tbsp chopped dill

3 tbsp plain flour

1 egg, beaten

100g panko breadcrumbs

4 tbsp sunflower oil

Salt and pepper to taste

Method
(SERVES 4)

Chilli and red pepper jam

1. Tip the peppers, chillies (with seeds), ginger and garlic into a food processor, then whiz until very finely chopped. Scrape into a heavy-bottomed pan with the tomatoes, sugar and vinegar, then bring everything to the boil. Skim off any scum that comes to the surface, then turn the heat down to a simmer and cook for about 50 minutes, stirring occasionally.

2. Once the jam is becoming sticky, continue cooking for 10-15 minutes more, stirring frequently so that it doesn't catch and burn. It should now look like thick, bubbling lava. Cool slightly, transfer to sterilised jars, then leave to cool completely.

3. It will keep for 3 months in a cold, dark cupboard – refrigerate once opened.

Salmon fishcakes

1. Heat the grill. Place the potatoes in a pan of water and bring to the boil, cover, and cook for 12-15 minutes until tender. Drain and leave to steam dry, then mash. Meanwhile, season the salmon and roast for 7 minutes until just cooked. Cool for a few minutes, then break into large chunks.

2. Mix the potato, mustard, zest, herbs and some seasoning. Lightly fold in the salmon, taking care not to break it up too much. Shape into fish cakes.

3. Put the egg, flour and breadcrumbs into 3 shallow dishes. Dip the cake in the flour, dust off any excess, then dip in the egg, and finally coat in breadcrumbs. Heat the oil in a large pan, then fry the cakes over a medium-low heat for 3-4 minutes each side until deep golden and heated through. Serve with lemon.

Salmon fishcakes, made well, are a delight. Far too often they are potato cakes with a bit of fish in – yuk! Add a little more lemon and pepper if like me your taste buds are slowly dying from abuse and old age!

Mouclade

Ingredients

2kg mussels
10g rock salt
2 shallots
1 garlic clove
2 egg yolks
1tsp curry paste
20cl white wine
100g crème fraiche
1g salt

Method
(SERVES 4)

1. Pre heat oven to 200C.

2. Place mussels in cold water, add rock salt and leave for 10 minutes, then clean the mussels.

3. Peel and finely chop the shallots and garlic.

4. Melt the butter in a pan then add the shallots and garlic. When the shallots are translucent, add the white wine and mussels and cook with a lid on for 2 minutes.

5. Strain the cooking juices and add the curry paste, egg yolks and cream then reduce by half. Once reduced, place the mussels in a dish and pour over the sauce. Bake in the oven for 4 minutes.

6. Serve immediately.

A simple dish, but one that flew out of the Flots Bleus in the 1960s – I love a touch of curry powder to chowders or vegetable soups alike – as you get older, your taste buds weaken, and I have become addicted to pepper and curry powder. The hotter the better! If you want to make this dish easier to eat, deshell the mussels before serving. Or just leave a third in shells for decoration.

Monkfish and prawn risotto

Ingredients

Tarragon butter
100g Welsh butter
40g tarragon, well chopped
Half a tsp of salt

Crab cakes
2cm piece of fresh root ginger, peeled
2 red chillies, seeds removed
250g white crab meat
1tbsp roughly chopped fresh coriander
2 spring onions, finely sliced
2 free-range eggs
7-8tbsp breadcrumbs
Plain flour for dusting
25ml olive oil

Risotto
2 onions, diced
250g Arborio rice
½ fennel bulb, diced
Zest and juice of one lemon
150g butter
Fish stock
Basil
Tarragon
Semi dried tomatoes
Red pepper, finely diced

Method
(SERVES 4)

Tarragon butter

1.   Soften the butter at room temperature and mix all the ingredients together in a food processor until well combined and green. Roll into sausages in cling film and keep in the fridge until needed.

Crab cakes

1.   Place the ginger and chilli into a mini food processor and pulse until finely chopped. In a bowl, combine the chilli and ginger with the white crabmeat, coriander, and spring onions. Crack in one egg and mix well, then stir in 4tbsps of the breadcrumbs.

2.   Divide the crab cake mixture into 6 equal portions and mould into patties. Place on a tray and chill in the fridge for about 20 minutes before cooking.

3.   Preheat the oven to 180C. Beat the remaining egg in a small bowl with 1tbsp of water to make an egg wash. Place some plain flour and the remaining breadcrumbs in separate shallow dishes.

4.   Dredge a crab cake in the flour, then dip into the egg and coat in the breadcrumbs. Shake gently to remove any excess breadcrumbs. Repeat with the remaining crab cakes.

5.   Heat the olive oil in a frying pan and fry the crab cakes for 2-3 minutes on each side, or until crisp and golden brown all over. Transfer the crab cakes to a baking tray and bake for 5-10 minutes, or until piping hot all the way through.

Risotto

1.   Add the chopped onion to a pan and fry for 5 minutes, until soft. Add rice and dry cook for 2 minutes. Add a splash of white wine and cover with fish stock. Cook until the rice softens, adding more stock as needed. Fry the fennel in a separate pan, then add peppers and tomatoes, lemon zest, basil, tarragon and risotto. Take off the heat and finish with butter and lemon juice to taste.

For the fish

1.   Roast the monkfish and prawns in tarragon butter on 140C for 7/8 minutes until cooked, season to taste.

This is a delightful risotto in my opinion with some of the finest food the sea can offer.

Lobster risotto

Ingredients

Risotto

2 onions, diced
250g Arborio rice
½ fennel bulb, diced
80g blanched spinach,
chopped
Zest and juice of one
lemon
150g butter
Fish stock
Asparagus
Chives
Black truffle
Capers

Crab cakes

80g cream
40g butter
40g four, plus extra for
coating
250g white crab meat
½ lemon
Basil
Salt and pepper
Panko breadcrumbs
1 egg, beaten

Method
(SERVES 4)

Lobster

1.   Boil a lobster for 20 mins, less if small. Cut in half and remove from shell, place one half down on a kedgeree dish. The meat from the claws can be used in a lobster cocktail

Risotto

1.   Add the onion to a pan and fry for 5 minutes until soft. Add rice and dry cook for two minutes. Add a splash of white wine and cover with fish stock. Cook until rice softens, adding more stock if needed. Fry fennel in a separate pan, then add spinach, lemon zest, chives and asparagus. Take off the heat and finish with butter and grated truffle and capers.

Crab cake

1.   Melt butter in a pan then add the flour. Slow cook for at least five minutes until flour has cooked out. Add the cream, then take off the heat and cool slightly. Add the white sauce to the crab, chopped basil and lemon. Season to taste. Form into balls, coat with flour, then egg and roll in breadcrumbs. Deep fry until golden brown.

This dish was created by Tom Simmons, a very creative chef of a few years ago – and soon to open his own restaurant in London, good luck! The dish encompasses everything that is good about summer eating by the coast. Pick a little samphire from the Pembrokeshire coast and decorate the dish with it, yummy.

Lobster Thermidor

Ingredients

1x750g/1 ½ lb lobster,
cooked
20g/ ¾ oz fresh parmesan,
grated

For the sauce
30g/ 1oz butter
1 shallot, finely chopped
1x284ml/ 10fl oz tub fresh
fish stock
55ml/ 2fl oz white wine
100ml/ 3 ½ fl oz double
cream
½ tsp English mustard
2 tbsp chopped parsley
½ lemon, juice only
Salt
Freshly ground black
pepper

Preparation method
(SERVES 2)

1. Cut the lobster in half and remove the meat from the claws and tail. Leave to one side. Remove any meat from the head and set aside. Cut the meat up into pieces and place back into the shell.

2. For the sauce, put the butter in a pan, add the shallots and cook until softened. Add the stock, wine and double cream and bring to the boil. Reduce by half. Add the mustard, herbs, lemon juice and seasoning.

3. Pre-heat the grill and spoon the sauce over the lobster meat. Sprinkle with the grated parmesan cheese. Place the lobster halves under a pre-heated grill for 3-4 minutes until golden brown.

This dish was very popular in the 60s and still is. The meat from the claws can be added to the bulk of the meat to create a larger portion – which is what I would do – rather than keep the claw meat for another dish!

Cockle and leek gratin

Ingredients

Cockle and leek gratin

2 leeks
40g butter
500g cockles
2tbsp of parsley
½ litre chicken stock
½ litre double cream
250g llangloffan cheese
½ lemon juice

Laverbread loaf

300g wholemeal flour
200g white bread flour
30g unsalted butter, plus
extra to serve
2tbsp fresh yeast
2tbsp oat bran
1tsp dark brown sugar
1tsp salt
Oil
285ml water
150g fresh laverbread

Method
(SERVES 6)

Cockle and leek gratin

1. Place the chicken stock and double cream in a large pan and reduce until it reaches a thick-sauce consistency.

2. Add cheese to the sauce and stir in well. Keep warm.

3. Slice leeks very finely and wash thoroughly. Chop the parsley.

4. In a pre-heated pan, sauté the leeks with butter until tender. Add the cockles and parsley and then combine with the sauce. Finish with the lemon juice and add salt and pepper to taste.

5. Place into gratin dishes and allow mixture to cool.

6. Top the gratins with breadcrumbs and grated Llanglofan cheese before roasting.

7. Roast for 7 minutes at 175C.

Laverbread loaf

1. To start the wholemeal loaf, combine the flours, butter, yeast, oat bran and sugar in the bowl of an electric mixer, fitted with a dough hook.

2. Add 285ml of water and the laverbread then mix on the lowest setting until a dough is formed. Continue mixing for 5-6 minutes, then add the salt and mix for a further minute.

3. Place the dough in a floured bowl cover with a clean damp tea towel and set aside in a warm, dry and draught free place for 2 hours, or until the dough has risen and doubled in size. Knock back and divide into a loaf tin.

4. Allow to rise and bake on 220C for 25 minutes or until hollow sounding when tapped on the bottom.

This dish serves well as a starter or a lunch dish with salad, or as an accompaniment to a main course. A great 'sense of place' dish. It was created by Tom Bennet, an inventive chef, and I love it.

Smoked haddock roulade

Ingredients

2 fillets of naturally dyed smoked haddock

350ml milk

1 bay leaf

A few black peppercorns

25g butter

25g plain flour

3 boiled eggs, 8 minutes, chopped

4 eggs, separated

1 small tin sweetcorn, drained

Salt and pepper

Method
(SERVES 6)

Roulade

1. Heat the milk, bay leaf and peppercorns in a saucepan and add the smoked haddock then cook for 4 minutes. Remove from the heat and leave to cool. When cold, strain off the milk and pick through the haddock, discarding the skin and bones and flaking the fish as you go.

2. Mix the egg yolks through the flaked fish and whisk the egg whites until fairly stiff, but not dry. Fold through the fish and season with ground pepper.

3. Spread the fish onto a baking tray lined with baking parchment until fairly flat. Bake for 10 – 12 minutes at 160°C or until the roulade is just springy.

4. Turn on to a clean tea towel topped with baking parchment and allow to cool. Remove the baking parchment that the haddock was cooked on.

Filling

1. Melt the butter and add the flour and cook out for 2-3 minutes, slowly adding enough of the haddock poaching milk to make a thick white sauce. Adjust the seasoning. Fold in the sweetcorn and boiled eggs and spread onto the roulade base.

2. Roll into a 'Swiss roll' style using the tea towel to roll it. Wrap in foil and leave to chill.

3. When needed, cut a thick slice and place into a small serving dish of a similar size. Moisten with 2tbsp of cream and bake for 8 – 10 minutes or until the cream coagulates.

A dish that used to be a regular on our menu in the 70s and 80s but seems to have lost favour by the modern day chef. Still, a great lunchtime meal and tasty. You can of course do a lot of versions; smoked salmon and salmon, or spinach roulade with a creamy mushroom filling, which is another we did.

Kedgeree

Ingredients

2 eggs
680g smoked haddock
fillets
2 bay leaves
170g long grain rice
Sea salt
110g butter
Thumb sized piece of fresh
ginger
1 onion
2 tbsp curry powder
1 tbsp mustard seed
2 tomatoes
Lemon juice
Chopped coriander
1 fresh red chilli
Natural yoghurt

Method
(SERVES 4)

1. Boil the eggs and cool.

2. Put the haddock and bay leaves in a pan with enough water
to cover, bring to the boil, cover and simmer for 5 minutes.
Cool, remove skin and flake.

3. Cook the rice and drain.

4. Melt the butter and soften the garlic, ginger and onion in a
pan. Add curry powder and mustard seeds, then add tomatoes
and lemon juice.

5. Chop the eggs, add the fish and rice and heat through.
Add the eggs, most of the coriander and chilli and stir. Mix the
remaining coriander and yoghurt and serve with the kedgeree.

This is a dish from my youth which I loved. But
you rarely see it on menus of today. It's one of
those 'Posh' dishes brought back from India by
the colonials at the turn of the century. P.O.S.H
is a relatively modern word derived from 'port
out, starboard home'. It was more expensive to
travel to India and back looking at land rather
than just gazing out to sea!

Poached fillet of hake, saffron mash, king prawns, tomato & Parma ham salsa

Ingredients

Hake
4 x 200g thick cut fillets of hake

Saffron mashed potato
1kg red rooster potatoes,
peeled and diced into 2-inch
pieces
2.5lt water
200ml double cream
150g Welsh butter
1 tsp saffron strands
Salt and pepper to taste

Poaching liquid
300ml water
2bay leaves
1 shallot – sliced
½ head of fennel – sliced
6 black peppercorns

King prawns
8 king prawns
50g butter
1 garlic clove – crushed
Juice of half a lemon

Tomato & Parma ham salsa
16/20 cherry tomatoes – halved
4 slices Parma ham cut in to
ribbons
1tsp chopped tarragon
3tbsp olive oil

Sauce
300ml fish stock
100ml white wine
Pinch of Saffron
30g butter

Decoration
2 red chillies – halved

Method
(SERVES 4)

Tomato & Parma ham salsa

1.   Coat the cherry tomatoes in olive oil and roast in the oven for 10 minutes to soften, leave to cool. Mix with the Parma ham, tarragon, salt and pepper and set aside.

Saffron mashed potato

1.   Add one tsp of salt to water in a deep pan and bring to the boil. Once boiling add the potatoes and boil for 20/25 minutes until tender. Strain through a colander and leave to air dry for 5 minutes until fluffy. Place the cream, butter and saffron in a pan and let it infuse over a low heat for 5 minutes. Once the potato is dry, pass through a drum sieve and then repeat once more. Place back into a deep pan and place back on a low heat, add the cream, butter and saffron and mix well. Season to taste, and serve.

Poaching liquid

1.   Put all the poaching liquid ingredients into a pan and bring to a simmer for 30 minutes to infuse.

Sauce

1.   Reduce the white wine down to half, add the fish stock and saffron and reduce until it starts to get syrupy. Take off the heat and stir in the butter.

King Prawns

1.   For the king prawns, heat the butter in a frying pan with the crushed garlic until foaming. Sauté the king prawns for 1-2 minutes, take off the heat and add the lemon juice.

Hake

1.   Gently poach the hake in the poaching liquid for 4-5 minutes, drain and keep them warm.

Assembly

1.   Griddle the chillies until coloured on the inside edges.

2.   Start with a couple of rochers of saffron mash. Add the hake and garnish with king prawns, tomato salsa and chillies. Flood the plate with the sauce.

We are lucky living by the sea with so much fresh fish available and hake is one of my favourites. Served with saffron mash it's yummy!

Pan-fried hake, tomato salsa, asparagus, hazelnut crumb, samphire

Ingredients

800g hake fillet
16 spears asparagus
100g butter
1.5kg Rooster potatoes
5 large vine tomatoes
200g samphire
1 bunch spring onions
1 lemon
2 tbsp olive oil
100g hazelnuts
½ tub laverbread
Salt and pepper to taste

Method
(SERVES 4)

1. Peel the potatoes and boil in salted water until just cooked. Drain and mash through a fine sieve or ricer and spread on a tray. Leave to cool.

2. Toast the hazelnuts in a hot pan for 5 minutes then place in a cloth and bash with a rolling pin.

3. Trim the hake fillet, and cut in to 4 equal portions, rinse and pat dry.

4. Peel or pick the leaves off the asparagus and cut to length.

5. De-seed the tomato and dice into 3mm cubes. Finely slice the spring onions and zest and juice the lemon. Combine with the olive oil and season with a little salt and pepper.

6. Pick any woody bits off the samphire grass and wash.

7. Put the laverbread in a sauce pan with the butter on a low heat until it dries out and starts to stick to the pan, add the mash and stir until it looks glossy and smooth.

8. In a medium heat frying pan add a little oil then sear the seasoned hake fillets, skin side first.

9. Quickly blanch the asparagus and samphire in salted boiling water.

10. Lay the tomato mix on a plate, placing the asparagus and samphire on top, then place on the hake fillets skin side up, finally sprinkling the hazelnut crumb on top, and serve.

Lovely colours with fresh and light ingredients – such a great summer eat, and of course virtually any fish could be used!

Pan-seared Pembrokeshire scallops, apple, celeriac puree

Ingredients

3 scallops per portion
Chickweed to garnish
Clarified butter

Celeriac puree
1 medium celeriac head, peeled and roughly chopped
75ml double cream
25g butter
1tsp lemon juice
Salt and pepper to season

Soy dressing
25g sliced shallots
130ml olive oil
Salt and pepper to season
2 springs fresh thyme
10ml soy sauce
25g beef glace
5ml truffle oil

Method
(SERVES 4)

1.   For the celeriac puree, cover the celeriac with water and add 1 tsp salt. Boil until very soft, then strain through a fine sieve to extract as much liquid as possible. Heat the cream and melt the butter. Put the cream, butter, celeriac and lemon juice into a blender and puree until completely smooth, and season to taste.

2.   For the soy dressing, sweat the shallots in 30ml of olive oil, add a pinch of salt and lightly colour. Add the thyme and sweat for another 2 minutes. Add the soy sauce and reduce to a syrup, then add the truffle oil and reduce by half. Add the beef glace and bring to the boil. Place the dressing into a blender and blend to a fine puree. Warm 100ml of olive oil and add to the puree. Place in a plastic bottle and keep at room temperature.

3.   For the scallops, put the clarified butter in a frying pan until hot. Add the scallops, turning once until browned on both sides (1-2 minutes). Remove from the heat and place on a paper towel.

4.   Place the elements onto a plate and garnish with granny smith apple, cut into matchsticks.

Scallops quickly cooked in a hot pan are delicious, use hand dived ones if you want to eat like a king, they cost about £3.00 each so it's not a cheap dish!

Duo of crab

Ingredients

Crab filo

1 egg
1 tsp mayonnaise
60g crab meat
½ lemon, zest and juice
Basil
Salt and pepper
4 sheets of filo pastry

Brown crab brioche

50g brioche, cubed
60g brown crab meat
20g cream
2g ground coriander
2g tarragon
40g whole egg
Salt

Cucumber fluid gel

200g cucumber juice
40g caster sugar
6g lemon juice
2g agar agar

Method
(SERVES 4)

Crab filo

1.   Some crab is held back to form a quenelle of crab, with horseradish mayonnaise, seasoning and a squeeze of lemon.

2.   Mix the mayonnaise, crab meat, zest and juice of a lemon with the basil and season to taste.

3.   Cut the filo into 20cm square pieces and layer in 3s. Place 1 heaped tbsp of crab mix onto the filo, rolling from the corner. Roll once and fold in the corners. Place the egg in a bowl and beat well. Using a pastry brush, brush the egg around the rest of the filo and roll the rest to seal, making sure the egg mix has stuck the seal down well. Leave to dry in the fridge for 2 minutes. Fry in a deep fat fryer on 180°C until golden brown. Halve and serve warm.

Brown crab brioche

1.   Add the brown crab and cream together in a deep pan, heat to 85°C. Add the coriander and tarragon and infuse to 10 minutes.

2.   Add the whole eggs and blitz until smooth. Season to taste and refrigerate.

3.   When needed, dip the brioche cubes in the mix until well covered and then fry in a non-stick frying pan until golden brown on each side. Serve immediately.

4.   Use chickweed and pea shoots to garnish.

Charcoal cucumber

1.   Quarter a cucumber and char in a hot dry pan until golden .Leave to cool and serve.

Cucumber fluid gel

1.   Blitz cucumber in a blender then pass through a fine sieve to make 200g of liquid. Add lemon juice and sugar. Immediately separate the mixture in half. Add agar agar to ½ the mixture and simmer for 2 minutes. Combine with the other ½ and pour into a container to set

Pembrokeshire and crab is just the best combination. There is a little work in this dish, but it is so, so lovely!

VEGETARIAN

Moroccan roast veg salad with goat's cheese

Ingredients

4 young carrots
2 fennel
8 baby turnip
6 baby beetroot
2 parsnips
2 shallots
1tsp cumin seeds
2 star anise
1tsp fennel seeds
1/2 cinnamon stick
1tsp sesame seeds
400ml orange juice
Agar-agar
150ml honey
50ml white wine vinegar
60g goat's cheese
200ml olive oil
Lettuce
Pumpkin seeds

I love the colours in the dish, it's a joy to bring to the table.

Method
(SERVES 4 AS A MAIN OR 8 AS A STARTER)

Fennel

1. Quarter the fennel bulbs and peel and quarter the shallots. Place into a pot with orange juice, star anise, fennel seeds, the cinnamon stick and half the coriander seeds. Cover with foil and braise until the fennel is well cooked. Set aside the fennel and shallots and pass the cooking liquid through a sieve. Set aside for later. Discard the spices.

Beetroot

1. Season and roast the beetroot until tender and slice into wedges.

Carrots

1. Peel and halve the carrots lengthways and marinade in olive oil with coriander seeds and cumin seeds. Season the carrots before roasting in the oven until well cooked. Remove the oil and seeds from carrots and roast for a further 5 minutes with honey and sesame seeds. Keep the excess oil.

Parsnips

1. Peel and quarter the parsnips lengthways, gently roast in oven with olive oil, honey and salt. Keep excess oil.

Baby turnips

1. Roast in oven with olive oil and salt. Keep excess oil.

Salad dressing

1. Place the olive oil that has been set aside from cooking the vegetables in a blender, and add a further 200ml of oil, 150ml of honey, 200ml of fennel braising liquid, 50ml of white wine vinegar, salt and pepper, and blend dressing.

Orange fluid gel

1. In a pan heat up the remaining cooking liquid from the fennel with 1 tbsp of sugar and 1% agar-agar. Bring to a simmer and then decant liquid into a tray and allow to set in a fridge, blend into fluid gel.

2. Warm the vegetables in the oven and combine in a bowl with salad leaves, goat's cheese and dressing. Finish with fluid gel and pumpkin seeds.

Spring asparagus, baby gem salad and chard

Ingredients

20 small asparagus tips
4 poached egg
Small handful of green beans
Pinch of small capers
½ fennel
Small handful of peas
2 bay gem lettuce
6 new potatoes

Dressing
25ml balsamic vinegar
25ml honey
100ml olive oil
25ml red wine vinegar

Method
(SERVES 4)

1. Cut off the top of the fennel, thinly slice and simmer in pickle liquor (100ml each of sugar, vinegar and water). Cut off the ends of the asparagus, and trim. Cut the green beans in half on a slant.

2. Boil the potatoes until slightly soft, then quarter.

3. Add green beans and peas to boiling water for 3 minutes.

4. Cut the lettuce in half and colour in a lightly oiled pan.

5. Scatter the lightly buttered greens and potatoes onto the dish and sprinkle on the capers.

6. Place the asparagus around the side and position the poached egg.

7. Drizzle in dressing and add a pinch of sea salt and parsley.

As asparagus came into season, I asked 'Turkish', one of our chefs at the time to come up with a dish, and this is what he produced. It's really very nice, well worth the effort.

Wild mushroom and asparagus risotto, crispy hen's egg

Ingredients

Crispy hen's egg

4 duck or hen's eggs

Splash of milk

Panco bread crumbs

50g flour

Boiling water

Wild mushroom and asparagus risotto

1 small onion, peeled and finely chopped

2 sticks celery, trimmed and finely chopped

400g risotto rice

75ml white wine

Sea salt

Freshly ground black pepper

4 large handfuls of wild mushrooms (shitake, girolle, chestnut or oyster) cleaned and sliced

A few sprigs of fresh chervil, tarragon or parsley, leaves picked and chopped

Juice of one lemon

1 tsp butter

1 small handful parmesan cheese, freshly grated

Extra virgin olive oil

1.5 ltrs organic vegetable stock, hot

4 asparagus tips chopped into pieces

Olive oil

Method
(SERVES 4)

Hen's egg

1.   Boil duck or hen's egg for 5 minutes and then cool in iced water as fast as possible. Peel the egg then roll in seasoned flour, then in egg and milk, then into panco bread crumbs. Refrigerate until needed. When required, deep fry on 180/200C for 1 – 1½ minutes until golden brown.

Risotto

1.   In a large pan, heat a lug of olive oil and add the onion and celery. Slowly fry without colouring them for at least 10 minutes, then turn the heat up and add the rice. Stir in the wine, keep stirring until the liquid has cooked into the rice. Add a good pinch of salt and your first ladle of hot stock. Turn the heat down to a simmer and keep adding ladles of stock, stirring and massaging the starch out of the rice, allowing each ladleful to be absorbed before adding the next.

2.   Carry on adding stock until the rice is soft but with a slight bite. This will take around 30 minutes. Meanwhile, get a dry griddle pan hot and grill the wild mushrooms until soft. If your pan isn't big enough, do this in batches. Put them into a bowl and add the chopped herbs, a pinch of salt and the lemon juice. Using a spoon mix everything together.

3.   Take the risotto off the heat and check the seasoning carefully. Stir in the butter and the parmesan. You want it to be creamy in texture, so add a bit more stock if you think it needs it. Put a lid on and leave the risotto to relax for about 3 minutes.

4.   Blanch your asparagus and add to risotto at the end.

5.   Take your risotto and add a little more seasoning or parmesan if you like. Serve a good dollop of risotto topped with some grilled dressed mushrooms, a sprinkling of freshly grated parmesan and a drizzle of extra virgin olive oil.

A spring dish to die for – look at the colour of the yolk of the Burford brown egg – a lovely starter or light snack.

Goat's cheese and red onion tart

Ingredients

Filling

6 tbsp balsamic vinegar

900g red onion, very finely sliced

100g goat's cheese

25g butter

1 level dessert spoon chopped fresh sage

8 sage leaves

A little olive oil

Cayenne for sprinkling

Salt and freshly milled black pepper

Cheese pastry

75g butter, room temperature

175g plain flour

50g strong cheddar cheese, grated

½ level tsp mustard powder

Pinch cayenne

1 egg, beaten

Method
(SERVES 8)

1. Pre heat oven to 180C, gas mark 4

2. First, make up the pastry by rubbing the butter lightly onto the flour, then adding the cheese, mustard and cayenne plus just enough cold water to make a smooth dough. Place the dough in a polythene bag to rest in the refrigerator for 20 minutes.

3. After that, roll it out as thinly as possible and use a 5 inch (13cm) cutter, or a saucer or something similar, to stamp out 8 rounds.

4. Line the greased tins with them, then bake in the oven, on the centre shelf, for 15-20 minutes or until the pastry is cooked through but not coloured. Then cool the pastry cases on a wire rack and store them in an airtight tin until they are needed.

5. To make the filling, melt the butter in a heavy-based, medium-sized saucepan. Stir in the onions, balsamic vinegar and chopped sage, season and let everything cook very gently without a lid, stirring often, for about 30 minutes until they have reduced down and taken on a lovely glazed appearance and all the excess liquid has evaporated away.

6. Then let the mixture cool until you are ready to make the tarts.

7. To bake them, brush a little beaten egg on to each pastry case, pop them back into the oven at the same temperature as above for 5 minutes; this helps to provide a seal for the pastry and prevents it becoming soggy.

8. Now spoon the onion mixture into the cases. Top each one with a slice of goat's cheese and a sage leaf that has first been dipped in olive oil.

9. Finally, sprinkle with a little cayenne and bake for 20 minutes.

Melt-in-your-mouth cheesy pastry, coupled with a blend of goat's cheese and red onions makes a delicious tart. It's popular with vegetarians or as a wholesome lunch with a dressed salad.

Molly Parkin

Ingredients

800g tinned tomatoes
2kg sliced parsnips
Salt and pepper to taste
550ml double cream
2 tbsp tomato puree
75g butter
Grated cheese with
breadcrumbs for topping.

Method
(SERVES 4)

1.   Put all ingredients in a pan and simmer until soft, about 50 minutes.

2.   Then, transfer into a dish and on top put the grated cheese and breadcrumbs.

3.   Put in the oven for about 15 minutes until brown.

4.   It's as simple as that. Don't imagine that the simplicity of the dish means it's lacking in flavour, it's anything but. It's a crackerjack recipe that's packed with great taste and is simple to prepare.

I would be a very rich man if I had a pound for every time I was asked for this recipe. Steve Brown, my head chef of some 20 years and now the sous chef in the kitchen, started serving this dish in the early 80s, and, I admit, it is a great eat and we have to serve it every Christmas with our turkey at functions to avoid a riot!

Spanakopita

Ingredients

2 packets filo pastry

50g butter and 50ml oil melted together

3 bags baby spinach leaf, wilted, roughly chopped

4 onions diced and fried

200g button mushrooms, quartered and fried

150g diced feta

8 eggs

½ litre milk

½ litre cream

Pinch nutmeg

Salt and pepper

Method
(SERVES 4)

1.   Mix the onions, mushrooms and spinach together.

2.   Beat the eggs, then add the milk, cream, nutmeg and salt and pepper and stir into the mushroom mix.

3.   Line a square 10' x 2' deep tin with filo (4 layers overlapped) brushed with the oil and butter mix.

4.   Fill the filo with the mushroom mix and dot the feta evenly in it. Top with 4 more layers of filo, and put in the oven on 160C for approximately 45 minutes.

We serve this dish at most of our weddings on the evening buffet/bbq. It is a great eat, and always complimented – providing of course you like spinach, mushrooms and feta cheese!

Butternut squash risotto, cooked walnuts, sage leaves

Ingredients

150g arborio rice
1 small onion, finely diced
1 butternut squash
50g parmesan, grated
25g candied walnuts, halved
50g sugar
50ml water
1/2tsp salt
sage leaves
150g butter
Approximately 1 litre of vegetable stock

Method
(SERVES 4)

1. Peel the butternut squash, halve and deseed, and chop the top half into small dice. Chop the remaining squash into rough dice and cook in a saucepan with 50g butter until tender. Put into a food processor and blend until smooth.

2. Put the sugar, salt and water into a saucepan and boil until a light syrup. Put the walnuts into the syrup and leave for 2 minutes, then drain off onto a non-stick baking mat and bake in a moderate heated oven until caramelised.

3. Deep fry the sage leaves for a few seconds until crisp and season.

4. Fry the squash dice in 25g of the butter until tender.

5. Fry the onions in a saucepan with a little oil until translucent, add the rice and fry gently for 2 minutes. Start adding the vegetable stock a ladle at a time, stirring until the rice absorbs it. Continue until the rice is cooked but al dente. This will take varying amounts of vegetable stock depending on the rice that you use, and how you like your rice cooked.

6. Remove the risotto from the heat and stir in the squash puree, some of the diced squash, parmesan and 50g diced butter until all melted and combined, season to taste.

7. Divide between 4 bowls and garnish with remaining diced squash, walnuts and sage leaves.

The more astute of you may notice that the risotto is accompanied with parsnip beignets – should you wish to know how to make these, contact www.wolfscastle.com and we will send you the recipe!

DESSERTS AND DRINKS

Café gourmande

Ingredients

Chocolate Truffle Cake
Sponge Base Chocolate
Mousse Topping
Mousse Filling
100g caster sugar
100g dark chocolate
230g dark chocolate
10g cocoa powder
50ml double cream
230g milk chocolate
75g egg whites
25g butter
4 egg yolks
50g melted butter
50g caster sugar
50g egg yolk
1 pint whipped cream
65g dark chocolate
(soft peaks)

Orange Sorbet
275ml water
175g caster sugar
50ml Grand Marnier
6 oranges (juiced)

Fruit Jelly
450ml apple juice
1 sachet gelatin
200g mixed berries

Sticky Date Tiramisu
Sticky Toffee Pudding
25ml Amaretto
100ml butterscotch sauce
25g caster sugar
130g mascarpone cheese
50ml Tia Maria
250ml cream
Strong coffee
1 vanilla pod

Fruit tart
Crème patisserie
8oz sweet pastry
500ml milk
Vanilla pod
6 egg yolks
120g caster sugar
50g plain flour
2tsp corn flower

Method
(SERVES 4)

Chocolate Truffle Cake

1.   For the sponge base: melt the chocolate, whisk the eggs and cocoa and slowly pour the butter in, add to chocolate. Make meringue with the egg whites and sugar and fold into the chocolate, spread onto a tray and bake for approx 12mins (until firm to touch).

2.   For the mousse filling: melt the chocolate, whisk the eggs and sugar until double in size, add to the chocolate, fold in cream and spread on top of the base. For the chocolate mousse topping: melt together all ingredients and pour on top of the mousse and portion when set.

Fruit Jelly

1.   Melt gelatin with 6tsp of warm water, add juice and fill moulds. Add fruit and leave to set.

Sticky Date Tiramisu

1.   Whisk the cream-cheese and half the Tia Maria, vanilla and 25ml coffee and sugar until it forms soft peaks. To make the dipping liquid add the remaining coffee, Ameretto and Tia Maria. Pour some butterscotch and then soak the sticky toffee pudding in the liquid and place in the bowl followed by the cream, repeat until full and dust with cocoa powder.

Fruit Tart

1.   Line the tin with pastry and bake until golden. For the crème patisserie: whisk the eggs and sugar until pale. Add flour and corn flour followed by boiled milk with vanilla. Heat gently until thick, like custard. Chill and add to pastry. Decorate with berries and serve.

Orange Sorbet

1.   Make a stock syrup in a pan with the sugar and water. Add orange juice, Grand Marnier and lemon juice, chill then churn in an ice-cream maker.

We have started offering this so that 5 different sweets can be enjoyed. LUSH!

Apple crumble

Ingredients

Crumble

575g Bramley apples
3 medium Granny Smiths,
peeled, cored and sliced to
1 cm thick
2 tbsp golden caster sugar
50g demerara sugar
50g caster sugar
1 pinch of cinnamon

Topping

100g flour
100g ground almonds
100g softened butter

Crème Anglaise

250ml cream
1 vanilla pod
4 egg yolks
70g caster sugar

Method
(SERVES 6)

1.   In a pan, add all the apples and sugar with a pinch of cinnamon and heat the apples until they become tender and the sugar has dissolved, then place into a baking dish.

2.   For the topping, add the flour, ground almonds and butter into a bowl, and mix together until you get clusters. Once achieved, break and sprinkle the topping over the apple mix until covered.

3.   Bake on 170C until a golden brown topping is achieved.

4.   For the crème Anglaise, heat the cream and vanilla in a pan until it bubbles around the edge. While the cream is heating, whisk together the yolks and sugar. Now pour the cream slowly into the egg mix, constantly whisking. Pour the mix back into the pan and place on a low heat, stirring constantly until it coats the back of a spoon.

5.   Pour the crème Anglaise over the crumble, and serve.

Childhood memories. To this day, I still love a good apple crumble – it's a winter comfort dessert at its best!

Sticky toffee pudding

Ingredients

Sticky toffee pudding
18oz soft brown sugar
6oz butter
3 eggs
1½ lb self-raising flour
1½ pts boiling water
3tsp raising agent
18oz dates
3tbsp vanilla essence

Vanilla ice cream
284ml double cream
300ml milk
115g caster sugar
1 vanilla pod
3 large egg yolks

Method
(SERVES 4)

Sticky toffee pudding

1. Chop the dates and soak with boiling water.

2. Whisk the eggs and sugar until pale. Add dates and liquid, followed by vanilla, flour and raising agent until well mixed and it looks like batter.

3. Pour into mould and bake on 170C until a skewer comes out clean. You can of course just pour into a dish and portion it at the end.

Ice cream

1. Bring the cream, milk and vanilla pods to the boil. Meanwhile whisk the egg yolks and sugar until pale. Whisk in the warm ream and allow to cool slightly. Put in the churner.

I can't remember when we started making this, but it was a long time ago for sure! Made well, as we do, it is a moorish sweet to die for!

Chocolate fondant

Ingredients

200g caster sugar
200g plain flour
4 eggs
4 egg yolks
200g dark chocolate

Method
(SERVES 6)

1.   Place the chocolate over a pan of simmering water to slowly melt mean while whisk the sugar and eggs in a bowl till it goes pale and double in size, pour in the flour and whisk again. Once the chocolate has melted add to the egg mixture and fold gently till well incorporated, butter 6 moulds with softened butter and dust with cocoa powder. Pour in the mixture leaving 1cm gap to allow for the dessert to rise.

2.   Pre-heat the oven on 180C and cook the fondants for around 10 minutes, once cooked tip out onto a plate and serve with your desired flavour of ice-cream.

Who doesn't like a fondant? Gooey chocolate oozing out from a divine chocolate sponge – chocolate heaven!

Vanilla cheesecake

Ingredients

Vanilla cheesecake

100g digestive biscuits or cookies crushed into fine crumbs

60g butter

500g full-fat cream cheese

100g icing sugar

1 vanilla pod, sliced lengthways, or 1 tsp vanilla extract

200ml double cream, lightly whipped

Blackberry jelly

200g frozen/fresh blackberries

75g caster sugar

50ml water

1 gelatine soaked in water till soft

Apple sorbet

750g Granny Smith apples

1 lemon, juiced

500ml water

350g caster sugar

4/5tbsp Calvados

Food colouring, optional

Method
(SERVES 6-8)

Vanilla Cheesecake

1.   In a mixing bowl, mix together the biscuit crumbs and the melted butter. Mix well.

2.   Spoon the biscuit mixture into your desired cake tin, which should be lined with silicon paper or baking parchment. Use a metal spoon to press the biscuit crumbs down firmly and evenly. Chill in the fridge until set.

3.   In a large mixing bowl, using a whisk or wooden spoon, beat together the cream cheese, icing sugar and vanilla pod seeds or vanilla extract until well mixed. Add the cream, which has been whipped to soft peaks.

4.   Spoon the cream mixture over the chilled biscuit base, making sure that there are no air bubbles. Smooth the top of the cheesecake with a palette knife or metal spoon and set in the fridge.

Blackberry jelly

1.   Place the blackberries into a bowl with the sugar. Covering with cling film and place over a Bain Marie to help release the blackberry juices.

2.   Once done, strain the juices and place into a pan with the gelatine and gently heat until warm. (1 sheet of gelatine will usually make around 250ml of jelly, depending on the strength).

3.   Leave to chill until just about to set. Pour on top of the cheesecake and leave to set.

Apple Sorbet

1.   Add the sugar, lemon juice and water into a pan and bring to the boil until the sugar has dissolved. While the water mix is heating, juice the apples and set aside.

2.   Once the sugar has dissolved add the apple juice and Calvados and the food colouring, if using. Set aside to cool over an ice bath and churn in an ice cream machine. (If no ice cream churn available, whisk every 20 minutes until it sets).

We make all sorts of flavoured cheesecakes and they are all creamy and scrumptious – a great eat.

Galette Normandie

Ingredients

230g plain flour
230g butter
115g cornflour
115g icing sugar (for the shortbread)
8 Granny Smith apples
150g sultanas
120g caster sugar
200g icing sugar (for the icing)
5tsp water

Method
(SERVES 4)

1. For the shortbread add the flour, butter, cornflour and icing sugar into a bowl and combine until you get a dough. Roll out as thinly as you can achieve and cut 3 disks the size of your desired mould. Bake blind for 12/15 minutes at 150C until they start to colour.

2. While the biscuit is cooling, peel and cut the apples into quarters and slice. Add them to a pan with the caster sugar and sultanas and cook until the apples are coated in a syrup from the sugar and are tender.

3. To assemble, place one biscuit at the bottom of the mould and place a good layer of apples on top, pressing down to get rid of any air gaps. Add the following layer and finally add the last biscuit. Now bake for 8 minutes at 140C. Once done, take out and chill.

4. For the icing, add the water to the icing sugar to make a paste and spread on top of the dessert. Drag a knife though the paste to make a pattern, then leave to set in the fridge.

The important thing with this dish is to ensure your shortbread biscuit is thin, and you have plenty of filling. This is a dish I remember well in the 1960s and I loved it. We hadn't made this for years until starting the book – it was the perfect excuse to revisit it.

Crepe Suzette

Ingredients

100g plain flour
1tbsp caster sugar
2 eggs
Sunflower oil

For the sauce
100g butter
100g caster sugar
150ml orange juice
1 orange, zested
1 lemon, zested
3 tbsp Grand Marnier
2 tbsp Cognac

Method
(SERVES 4)

1. Put the flour, sugar and a pinch of salt in a large bowl. Make a well in the centre, add the eggs, oil and 2 tbsp of the milk and beat together with a wooden spoon until smooth. Slowly start to pour in a little milk, mixing as you pour, to keep the batter smooth. Pour in the rest of the milk, a bit more quickly now, until it looks like a single cream.

2. Heat a 15cm/6inch crepe pan. Measure 2½ tbsp of the batter into a jug, then pour into the pan, moving it around so the mixture swirls and fits the bottom of the pan. When the crepe is golden underneath (in about 15 seconds if the pan is the right temperature), turn and cook for a further 30 seconds, until spotted brown.

3. Slide the crepe on to a plate. Wipe the pan with oiled kitchen paper and continue frying until all the batter is used, stacking the crepes on top of each other as you cook them. You can freeze the pancakes at this stage, wrapped in cling film and foil. Or make a day ahead, wrap and keep in the fridge.

4. For the sauce, heat the butter and sugar in a deep frying pan (about 25cm/10inches) over a low heat, stirring occasionally, until the sugar begins to dissolve. Turn up the heat and bubble quite fast until the mixture just starts to go brown and caramelise (about 4 minutes), stirring only towards the end. Pour in the orange juice, add the orange and lemon zests, letting the mixture bubble for 3-4 minutes to thicken slightly. Add the Grand Marnier and Cognac, heat for a few seconds and lower the heat.

5. Put one crepe into the juices and holding it with a fork, coat it well in the mixture. Fold it into quarters and push to one side of the pan. Continue the coating and folding with the remaining pancakes. Serve 2-3 crepes per person with the sauce.

1968 – Blackpool catering college. For 7/6 (37 ½p) you could have a smoked salmon starter, followed by flambéed steak Diane, with Crepe Suzette to finish – it rose to 50p by the time I left – but what a bargain. Each table would be looked after by at least 2 waiters – virtually a ratio of 1 waiter per guest – not surprisingly the restaurant was always packed and you had to book at least 3 weeks in advance!

Strawberry bavarois

Ingredients

225g strawberries, hulled
50g icing sugar
120g caster sugar
50ml cold water
3 egg yolks
2 leaves of gelatine,
bloomed (softened in cold
water, then squeezed
gently to remove excess
water)
200g strawberry puree,
chilled
300ml whipping cream

**Dandelion and burdock
gel**

300g Fentimans dandelion
and burdock drink
75g caster sugar
3g agar agar

Strawberry macarons

71g ground almonds
Pinch of salt
117g icing sugar
2 large egg whites (room
temperature)
53g caster sugar
Food colouring of choice
50g soft butter
3tbsp strawberry jam

Method
(SERVES 6)

1. To make the bavarois, place the caster sugar, water and egg yolks in a large heatproof bowl over a pan of simmering water. Whisk the mixture continuously for about 12 minutes or until the mixture (sabayon) becomes thickened and pale yellow in colour. Remove from the heat, add the bloomed gelatine and whisk for about 30 seconds or until dissolved. Whisk in the chilled strawberry puree. Transfer the mixture to a clean bowl set over ice and leave to cool.

2. In a separate bowl, semi-whip the cream until it forms soft peaks. Fold the whipped cream into the strawberry bavarois mixture until combined. Transfer the mixture to a piping bag fitted with a large plain nozzle (or simply use a disposable piping bag and snip the end off to make a hole for piping). Pipe the bavarois mixture into the dessert glasses, dividing equally, and add the strawberries on top. Refrigerate for about 4 hours or until completely set. Once set, cover the glasses with cling film, if you are serving the desserts the next day.

3. Add the dandelion and burdock to a pan with the sugar and bring to the boil. Add the agar and mix well, leave to chill in the fridge until set. Once set, blitz in a food processor and pass through a sieve to ensure no lumps are present.

4. To make the macarons, sieve the ground almonds and icing sugar into a bowl and set aside. Place the egg whites into a bowl with the salt and whisk with the whisk attachment. Whisk until a meringue starts to form, then add the caster sugar and continue to whisk until stiff peaks form. Add the desired colour, using a little more if needed. In a bowl add the almonds and icing sugar you sieved earlier, folding with a rubber spatula, ensuring you don't over whisk, resulting in a runny mix (around 50 folds should be enough). Once done, pipe on to parchment paper and leave to form a skin for around 20 - 30 mins. Bake in a pre-heated oven at around 160C for 12/15 minutes. Once cool, add the butter and jam into a bowl and mix until light and fluffy. Transfer to a piping bag and divide on to one half of the macaron and then place another on top.

This is a great summer dessert which we feature at some time during each summer.

Thai marinated pineapple

Ingredients

Marinade for pineapple
1 green chilli
130g lemon grass
2 limes, zest and juice
80g coriander
12 cardamom pods
180g Malibu
280g palm sugar (grated)
2 pineapple

Doughnuts
115g strong bread flour
2g salt
25g fresh yeast
18g sugar
37g milk
25g egg yolk
15g butter, melted but
not hot

Cinnamon sugar
200g caster sugar
½ tsp cinnamon

Chocolate sauce
125ml water
80g glucose syrup
30g cocoa powder
100g caster sugar
30g dark chocolate

Coconut tuile
25g butter
40g desiccated coconut
40g icing sugar
13g plain flour
1 egg white

Cardamom ice cream
225g caster sugar
4 egg yolks
340ml milk
340ml double cream
2 tsp vanilla extract
10/12 cardamom pods,
finely grounded

RECIPE CONTINUES OVERLEAF

Method
(SERVES 6-8)

Marinade for pineapple

1. Roughly dice the lemon grass and chilli, removing the seeds. Extract the seeds from the cardamom pods. Place all of the ingredients in a food processor and blitz.

2. Remove the pineapple skin and outer layer and slice into 2cm thick circles removing the core with an apple corer. Place in a vac bag or container with the marinade. Seal tightly and leave for ½ a day.

Doughnuts

1. Mix the yeast, milk and half the sugar into a bowl, cover and leave in a warm place till frothy, add the flour, melted butter and egg into a bowl and mix, once done make a well in the flour and add the yeast mixture to form a dough then knead for 5 minutes, add back to a clean floured bowl and leave to prove until double in size.

2. On a floured surface knead the dough once again and divide into desired size keeping in mind they will double in volume, once the doughnuts have proved for the second time deep fry the doughnuts until golden brown and roll in the cinnamon sugar.

Chocolate sauce

1. Add the water, glucose and sugar to a pan and bring to a steady boil. Add the remaining ingredients and bring back to the boil, so that all the ingredients are well combined. Strain to remove any lumps, and leave to cool in the fridge.

Coconut tuile

1. Whizz the coconut in a food processor followed by the softened butter, icing sugar, flour and egg white. The mixture should be soft enough to spread, if not, leave to chill in a fridge. Once ready, cut out a desired mould from an old plastic lid and spread the mix leaving a template of your desired shape. Cook on 180C until golden brown and shape immediately if needed before the biscuit sets.

2. Once ready to assemble, spread some of the chocolate sauce on the bottom of the plate and place a piece of pineapple on top followed by 3 doughnuts and a tuile biscuit. Finish off by garnishing with a little baby coriander.

Cardamom ice cream

1. In a bowl whisk the egg yolks and sugar till pale, meanwhile place the rest of the ingredients into a pan and heat gently. Add the egg mixture and whisk on a gentle heat till you achieve a custard-like consistency, leave to cool so that the cardamom flavours infuse then pass through a sieve to remove the seeds and pour into an ice-cream machine and churn.

This is a great summer dessert with an eastern twist!

'Allt yr Afon' Tiramisu

Ingredients

Cream
100g icing sugar
530g mascarpone
100ml Tia Maria
1000ml double cream
1 shot espresso
2 vanilla pods

Sponge
Sticky toffee pudding, cut into slices, see Page 218
35ml Amaretto
35ml Tia Maria
300ml espresso

Butterscotch sauce
25g butter
50g soft brown sugar
75ml cream

Method
(SERVES 4)

1.   Add all the ingredients for the cream into a mixing bowl and whip until soft peaks form.

2.   In a glass, add a little butterscotch at the bottom, add some sticky toffee pudding dipped into the coffee mixture (espresso, Amaretto and Tia Maria mixed) on top, followed by some of the cream. Repeat until the glass is full with repetitive layers.

3.   Dust with cocoa powder and serve with Amaretti biscuits.

Butterscotch sauce

1.   Boil the ingredients for 2 minutes and leave to cool.

This is my dessert chef Mike Rees' version of a tiramisu, combined with sticky toffee pudding. I defy anyone not to like this dish, it is so moreish!

Black Forest gateau

Ingredients

Chocolate sponge
200g cherries, cherry liquor
100g caster sugar
20g cocoa powder
150g egg white
100g butter, melted and warm
100g egg yolk
125g 70% bitter chocolate

Vanilla and white chocolate mouse
100g white chocolate
1 gelatine leaf, softened in cold water
200g double cream
2 vanilla pods, split and seeds scraped
300g double cream, whipped to soft peaks

Method
(SERVES 4)

Chocolate sponge

1. Place the egg whites in the bowl of a food mixer with a whisk attached. Set to a medium/high speed and whisk until the egg whites start to increase in volume, then slowly add the sugar. Continue to whisk until the meringue has reached medium peaks.

2. Preheat the oven to 170C/gas mark 3-4. Meanwhile, melt the chocolate in a bain marie. In a separate bowl, sift the cocoa powder over the egg yolks, whisking thoroughly to combine. Slowly pour and continue to whisk in the melted butter. Remove from the heat and allow to cool before gently folding in the meringue, 1/3 at a time to incorporate as much air as possible.

3. Line a shallow baking tray with parchment and evenly spread out the chocolate sponge mix. Place into the oven for 10 minutes, then remove and allow to cool completely before handling.

4. Use a 6cm pastry cutter to make 8 rounds of the sponge. Use 4 of the sponge rings as the base and place into a high-sided 6cm pastry ring. Reserve the other 4 rounds until later.

Vanilla and white chocolate mousse

1. Pour 200ml of double cream into a pan with the vanilla. Bring to the boil and then remove from the heat.

2. Place the white chocolate into a bowl and pass the hot vanilla cream through a fine chinois onto the chocolate stirring to dissolve. Add the softened gelatine and whisk to combine. Set aside to cool slightly.

3. While the white chocolate mix is cooling, use a pastry brush to seal the chocolate sponge base in the kirsch, reserved from the griottine cherries. Once the chocolate mix is cool, fold in 300ml of whipped double cream. While still runny, pour the white chocolate mix over the soaked sponge to create a second layer, around 5mm in thickness.

4. Remove the pips from the griottine cherries, cut in half and place seven halves into each of the 4 rings on top of the white chocolate layer. Press down firmly so the white chocolate mixture fills out all the gaps between the two layers of sponge.

5. Use up any leftover liquid from the cherries to brush the top layer of chocolate sponge before pressing the top layer lightly down into the ring. Set in the refrigerator for up to 2 hours.

6. Once set, remove the gateau from the ring using a knife and roll in some chocolate flakes or crushed chocolate chips.

RECIPE CONTINUES OVERLEAF

Dark chocolate delice

350g dark chocolate buttons

200ml cream, whipped to soft peaks

100g egg yolk

50g caster sugar

250ml whole milk

250ml cream

Cherry gel

100g cherry puree

1g agar agar

Cherry sorbet

800g cherry puree

600g water

345g sugar

75g dextrose

75g glucose

3g ice cream stabiliser

Chantilly cream

300ml double cream

60g caster sugar

1 vanilla pod

Method

Dark chocolate delice

1.   Combine the cream and milk in a pan and bring to the boil. Meanwhile, whisk together the yolks and sugar in a large bowl until smooth and pale in colour.

2.   Slowly add the cream mixture to the yolks and sugar while whisking continuously. Return the liquid to the pan to make a crème Anglaise. Stir on the heat until it is thick enough to coat the back of a spoon. When it is ready, measure out 500ml and set aside.

3.   Melt the dark chocolate in a large bowl over a bain marie. While the crème Anglaise mix is still hot, slowly pour into the chocolate, in three parts, whisking as you go. Allow to cool to 37C.

4.   As the chocolate mixture is cooling to temperature, gently fold in the cream. Pour the mix into the gateau rings, covering the top layer of sponge. Allow to set for a minimum of 4 hours.

Cherry gel

1.   For the cherry gel, add the cherry puree to a pan and the agar agar and heat till it starts to bubble. Remove from the heat and pour into a bowl and chill in the fridge. Once set, blend in a food processor till smooth.

Chantilly cream

1.   Add the cream to a bowl with vanilla and sugar. Whisk till you get soft peaks and store in the fridge till needed.

Cherry sorbet

1.   Place the water, puree, sugars and stabilisers into a pan and heat to 75C. Let it sit for 15/20 minutes to hydrate the solids and stir again to smooth the mixture. Allow to cool to room temperature and process in an ice cream machine.

Such a popular dessert in the very early years – but of course then it was a slice of a large cake. This version has been modernised and is absolutely delicious.

Brandied bread and butter pudding

Ingredients

12 slices of white bread
125g softened butter
300g soft light brown sugar
150g sultanas
1 tsp ground cinnamon
100ml brandy
560ml double cream
6 large eggs
1tsp vanilla extract

Method
(SERVES 6-8)

1.   Butter the bread and trim off the crusts, cut each slice into 3 pieces.

2.   Butter a deep ceramic ovenproof dish approximately 20cm by 30cm.

3.   Arrange 1 layer of bread, sprinkle with a quarter of the sugar, a third of the sultanas, and some cinnamon.

4.   Repeat with 3 more layers and finish the top layer off with the remaining sugar and cinnamon.

5.   Lightly beat the eggs, cream, brandy and vanilla together.

6.   Pour gently over the layered bread, pressing the top layer into the custard mix with a fork.

7.   Leave to rest for half an hour before cooking at 220C/gas mark 5 for 30 minutes until the top is golden and the centre cooked.

8.   Allow to rest for a further 10 minutes before serving with custard, double cream or vanilla ice cream.

Hilary Rice who worked with us in the late 70s and early 80s, took this recipe with her and all the years she owned 'The Huntsman' restaurant in Dinas Powys this recipe featured on her menu. When she heard I was writing a cookery book, she sent it to me – so here it is!

Trio of desserts

Ingredients

Strawberry cheesecake
165g digestive biscuits
115g melted butter
200g strawberries, hulled
35g caster sugar
175ml double cream
340g cream cheese

Shortbread biscuit
110g plain flour
110g soft butter
55g icing sugar
55g corn flour
½ vanilla pod
Caster sugar for decoration

Coulis
300g strawberries, hulled
60g caster sugar
3g Agar Agar

Chocolate sorbet
200g cater sugar
50g cocoa powder
50g dark chocolate, finely chopped
1tsp vanilla essence
600ml water

Chantilly cream
200g whipping cream/ double cream
100g icing/caster sugar
1 vanilla pod

Chocolate decoration
100g dark chocolate

To make the sticky toffee pudding, see Page 218

Method
(SERVES 8)

Strawberry cheesecake

1. Blend the biscuits until fine and combine with the butter. Cover the base of a 6-inch springform tin and leave to chill in the fridge.

2. Puree the strawberries and sugar together. In a mixing bowl whisk the cream cheese and cream until smooth, add the strawberry puree and whisk until it thickens up.

3. Pour the mixture on top of the biscuit base and leave to set in a fridge overnight.

Shortbread biscuit

1. Add all the ingredients into a bowl and rub together to form a dough.

2. Roll out with a rolling pin till you achieve a 1cm thick dough and cut with a 4cm pastry cutter. Place on a tray lined with parchment paper and bake on 160 degrees centigrade for 15 minutes or till the dough starts to go golden brown round the edges.

3. Once done, sprinkle some caster sugar over the top and allow to cool.

Coulis

1. In a blender add the strawberries and sugar and blend until smooth.

2. Pour the mixture into a pan and add the Agar Agar and whisk on a low heat till it starts to bubble, Pour onto a tray and leave to set.

3. Once set, blitz in a blender until smooth and pour into a squeezy bottle.

Chocolate sorbet

1. Add the water, cocoa powder and sugar to a pan and bring to a gentle simmer for 5 minutes. Remove from the heat and add the chocolate and vanilla, whisk till the chocolate has melted and pass through a sieve.

2. Cool the mixture over a bowl of ice, then churn in an ice cream machine until a smooth frozen paste has formed. Add to a plastic tub and leave till required (his can be done a day in advance if needed).

Chocolate decoration

1.   Over a pan of boiling water, melt the chocolate in a heat proof bowl until melted. Pour into a piping bag and trim the end to your desired thickness. Pipe out your chosen design on to some baking parchment, and leave to chill in a fridge until needed.

Chantilly cream

1.   In a bowl, add the cream, vanilla and sugar and whisk until you get stiff peaks. Once done, store in the fridge until required.

A great little trio.

Chocolate brownie and fudge

Ingredients

Chocolate brownies
275g dark chocolate
275g unsalted butter
85g pecans, broken into
pieces
85g white chocolate
85g milk chocolate
175g plain flour
1 tsp baking powder
4 large eggs
2 tsp vanilla essence
325g caster sugar

Fudge
1kg granulated sugar
125g butter
450ml milk
450ml cream
50g liquid glucose
250g icing sugar

Method

Brownies

1.   Preheat oven to 170C.

2.   Line a tray with lightly buttered baking parchment.

3.   Put the plain chocolate and butter in a large bowl, place over a pan of simmering water and allow to melt.

4.   Sieve the flour and baking powder into a bowl and set aside.

5.   Remove the melted chocolate from the heat and stir in the sugar. Add the eggs and vanilla essence. Fold in the flour, nuts and chocolate, then pour into the prepared tray, and cook for 20 minutes or until slightly set in the middle.

Fudge

1.   Add the butter, cream, milk, glucose and sugar to the pan and bring to a gentle boil until it reaches 116-118C.

2.   Pour mixture into a mixing bowl and add the icing sugar and other desired flavouring and mix until it is well incorporated. Pour onto a lined tray and leave to set overnight, or until cold.

I think these are the best brownies you will ever eat, and the fudge, well, we've been offering it with coffee for 40 years! Occasionally, we do get bored of making it and try something else, but then the complaints come in – so – it's fudge for the next 40 years I suppose!

Cocktails

Ingredients

Blackberry and apple bramble
1½ shot Brecon gin
100ml apple juice
100ml appletizer
10 frozen blackberries
½ tsp sugar

Cosmopolitan
1 and ½ shots of vodka
½ shot of Cointreau
½ shot of lime juice
100ml cranberry juice

Method

Blackberry and apple bramble

1. Add everything but the Appletizer to a cocktail shaker and shake well.

2. Pour into a glass with ice, and finish with appletizer.

3. Decorate with a few blackberries.

An easy-to-make cocktail which will require a second tasting!

Cosmopolitan

1. Add all ingredients together in a cocktail shaker with ice, and shake well.

2. Serve in a Martini glass, and garnish with lime or orange peel.

As pre-dinner drinks, just divine, and you have to have 2. My grandmother always used to say when you offered her another drink, 'Well dear, a bird can't fly on 1 wing.' And who would argue with a 97 year old?!

Cocktails

Ingredients

Mojito
2 shots Bacardi rum
3 fresh limes
1 large handful of fresh mint (found in Andy's garden!)
2 tsp white sugar
1 shot lime cordial

Raspberry margarita
1 shot of tequila
1 shot of triple sec
½ shot of fresh lime juice
4 shots of raspberry coulis (homemade)
2 tsp white sugar

Method

Mojito

1. Cut all the limes into quarters, then squeeze the lime juice into a cocktail shaker.

2. Add all the mint then crush the mint and lime juice together. Add the sugar, lime cordial and rum, and shake rapidly.

3. Serve in a water glass over crushed ice, and garnish with a lime wedge and fresh mint.

Eleanor, who wrote this recipe, has put that you can find the mint in my garden, well, you can now! I've spent 3 years cultivating my mint patch and it finally has taken off, as we use a lot of mint for cocktails, flavouring potatoes, and Pimms for ladies' day. This is a day created by Nicky Gerson, daughter of Judy Kelly, a lovely, lovely lady who sadly died over 10 years ago of cancer. Nicky started the occasion to raise money for a local cancer charity. The day must have raised over £50,000 by now, and a lot of Pimms is drunk on the day – so we need plenty of mint, as, with Mojito's – mint is must!

Raspberry margarita

1. Add the ingredients into a cocktail shaker, and shake well.

2. Serve in a water glass over crushed ice, and use a lime wedge and fresh raspberries to garnish.

A hot summer's day, what else do you need, heaven in a glass!

Recipe index